B L A C K • W H I T E • A N D I N C O L O R

BLACK · WHITE · AND IN COLOR

TELEVISION AND BLACK CIVIL RIGHTS

by Sasha Torres

PRINCETON UNIVERSITY PRESS · PRINCETON AND OXFORD

Library of Congress Cataloging-in-Publication Data

Torres, Sasha.
Black, white, and in color : television and black civil rights / Sasha Torres.
p. cm.
Includes bibliographical references and index.
ISBN 0–691–01658–5 (alk. paper) — ISBN 0–691–01657–7 (pbk. : alk. paper)
1. African Americans on television.   2. Television broadcasting of news —
United States.   3. African Americans — Press coverage — History — 20th
century.   4. African Americans — Civil rights — History — 20th century.   I. Title.

PN1992.8.A34 T67 2003
070.1'95 — dc21   2002070400

British Library Cataloging-in-Publication Data is available

This book has been composed in Sabon Typeface

Printed on acid-free paper. ∞

www.pupress.princeton.edu

Printed in the United States of America

10 9 8 7 6 5 4 3 2

ISBN-13: 978-0-691-01657-3 (pbk.)

*For my father, John Torres, Jr., (1938–2001)
and Brian Selsky (1967–1997)*

Contents

Illustrations

Acknowledgments

$\mathbf{M}$ANY INSTITUTIONS, individuals, and collectivities have challenged and supported this work during the long process of its production. I have been the grateful beneficiary of research funding and writing time from the Freedom Forum's Media Studies Center, the Schomburg Center for Research in Black Culture, Brown University, and the Johns Hopkins University. More crucially, colleagues in each of the institutions have provided indispensable camaraderie; they include Chris Amirault, Nancy Armstrong, Douglas Chambers, Ying Chan, Nahum Chandler, Ken Dautrich, Howard Dodson, Brent Edwards, Frances Ferguson, Elizabeth Francis, Gerald Gill, Mike Godwin, Jonathan Goldberg, Maryemma Graham, Allen Grossman, Hank Klibanoff, Suzanne Braun Levine, Katrina Bell McDonald, Larry McGill, Michael Moon, Robert O'Meally, Nell Irwin Painter, Monroe Price, John Plotz, Richard Reeves, Robert Reid-Pharr, Deborah Rogers, Robert Scholes, Bryan Shepp, Robert Snyder, Leonard Tennenhouse, Leslie Thornton, and Irene Tucker. In addition, I have been fortunate to have received the superior research assistance of Chris Cagle, Jessica Crewe, Michael Kackman, Erin Matzen, Kendall Moore, and Bonnie Morrison. I am grateful as well for help from Richard Manning at the Brown University Film Archive; Ruta Abolins and Maxine Flexner-Ducy at the Wisconsin Center for Film and Theater Research; Madeline Matz of the Motion Picture, Broadcasting, and Recorded Sound Division at the Library of Congress; and Cynthia P. Lewis at the archive of the Martin Luther King, Jr., Center for Nonviolent Social Change.

A number of colleagues have read the manuscript, in whole or in part, and provided suggestions, criticism, and encouragement. I am thankful in particular to my editors, Deborah Malmud and later Mary Murrell, and to Lauren Berlant, Amanda Berry, Jacqueline Bobo, Frances Ferguson, Jonathan Flatley, Judith Frank, Allen Grossman, Phillip Brian Harper, Walter Benn Michaels, José Muñoz, Robert Reid-Pharr, Matthew Rowlinson, and Melissa Zeiger. In addition, audiences at Dartmouth College, Duke University, Harvard University, George Mason University, the Johns Hopkins University, the Modern Language Association, Northwestern University, Smith College, UCLA, and the University of Chicago have asked invaluably provocative questions during presentations of these chapters. Finally, the readers who reviewed the manuscript for Princeton University Press produced wonderfully useful reports: rigorous, encouraging, and practical. I am extremely grateful to them both.

Many, many others have provided other kinds of help, not so much perhaps in the work of making the book, but in the more important work of making a life. Members, past and present, of the editorial collective of *Camera Obscura* — Julie D'Acci, Phillip Brian Harper, Amelie Hastie, Lynne Joyrich, Elisabeth Lyon, Constance Penley, Patricia White, and Sharon Willis — remind me continually of the many values of intellectual work and never fail to provide tonic for flagging spirits or institutionally induced ennui. In addition, my everyday life has been blessed by the presence of Elizabeth Alexander, Jon Berenson, Mandy Berry, Stephen Best, Mollie Brooks, Maryellen Butke, Jonathan Crewe, Jennifer Doyle, Jon Flatley, Judy Frank, Allison Gaines, Simon Glick, Brian Goldberg, Joanne Gormley, Amy Hollywood, Alexis Jetter, Katie Kent, Annelise Orleck, Agnes Perry, John Plotz, Seska Ramberg, Christophora Robeers, Peggy Schjeldahl, Brian Selsky, Brenda Silver, Elisabeth Subrin, Lisa Soltani, Rebecca Sumner-Burgos, John Torres, Margaret Torres, and Ben Weaver.

I couldn't have finished this book without having been the student of some marvelous teachers. Jeff Nunokawa has instructed me in crucial lessons on writing and persistence. Candace Vogler has taught me what this book was about, among many other things. Eve Kosofsky Sedgwick and Melissa Zeiger continually train me in courage. Lauren Berlant reminds me that I'm possible. José Muñoz lovingly helps me keep track of my identifications and disidentifications. And Matthew Rowlinson — by sheltering me, and this book, through much of its composition — has taught belated lessons in object permanence.

An earlier version of chapter 3, "King TV," appeared in my edited work *Living Color: Race and Television in the United States* (Durham: Duke University Press, 1998), 140–60. Chapter 4 first appeared in *Zero Tolerance: Quality of Life and the New Police Brutality in New York City*, ed. Andrea McArdle and Tanya Erzen (New York: New York University Press, 2001), 85–103.

BLACK · WHITE · AND IN COLOR

Introduction

Scholarly accounts of racial representation in American television have been dominated by the conceptual category of the "stereotype." A good example — though one might cite many others — of this tendency is Jannette L. Dates and William Barlow's collection, *Split Image: African Americans in the Mass Media*, which treats many aspects of mass-mediated culture and contains several sections on television.[1] In the general theoretical introduction to the volume, Dates and Barlow trace a number of African American stereotypes back to their historical origins in antebellum popular culture, arguing that the versions persisting in contemporary commercial culture may be meaningfully linked to these origins in minstrelsy. For Dates and Barlow, widely circulated stereotypes such as the comic Negro, the Jim Crow figure, the pickaninny, the tragic mulatto, and the Aunt Jemima are perpetuated by whites in an effort to secure and maintain cultural power. The history of African American mass-mediated representation, then, is the history of a "split image," in which "the dominant trend in African American portraiture has been created and nurtured by succeeding generations of white image makers, beginning as far back as the colonial era," while "[i]ts opposite has been created and maintained by black image makers in response to the omissions and distortions of the former."[2] The intellectual and political purchase of accounts like Dates and Barlow's is considerable for a number of reasons. The stability of the white oppressor/black victim binary is always tempting, and often accurate. In addition, such readings have historically been successful in organizing aggrieved collectivities of (usually middle-class) African American spectators into counterpublics, as in the NAACP's campaign against the television version of *Amos 'n' Andy*.[3] Finally, these accounts are extremely efficient at replacing the pain of outrage and indignation with the pleasures of thinking "I know what that means."[4]

But the cost of these gains is rather high. First, these accounts leave little room for the complex, and often resistant, spectatorship engendered by the sheer egregiousness of such stereotypes, or for the creative and unpredictable cultural work it does. The NAACP's fifteen-year campaign against *Amos 'n' Andy*, for example, could not prevent a young Henry Louis Gates, Jr., and his black community in Piedmont,

West Virginia, from "loving" the show. In his memoir, *Colored People*, Gates recalls,

> *everybody* loved *Amos 'n' Andy*—I don't care what people say today. For the colored people, the day they took *Amos 'n' Andy* off the air was one of the saddest days in Piedmont. . . .
>
> What was special to us about *Amos 'n' Andy* was that their world was *all* colored, just like ours. Of course, *they* had their colored judges and lawyers and doctors and nurses, which we could only dream about having, or becoming—and we *did* dream about those things.[5]

While *Amos 'n' Andy* was inspiring dreams of becoming a doctor or lawyer in Piedmont, elsewhere in the segregated South it was giving the girl who would become bell hooks some of her early training in cultural criticism. She writes,

> a poor black family, like the one I was raised in, might sit around watching *Amos 'n' Andy*—enjoying it as we simultaneously critiqued it—talking about the ways this cultural production served the interests of white supremacy. We knew we were not watching representations of ourselves created by black artists or progressive white folks. Within the context of an apartheid social structure where practically every aspect of black life was determined by the efforts of those in power to maintain white supremacy, black folks were incredibly vigilant. . . . Watching television in the fifties and sixties, and listening to adult conversation, was one of the primary ways young black folks learned about race politics.[6]

Note that hooks's account focuses not on the stereotypes themselves, but on the interpretive community they generated, and the useful political effects of that interpretive work. Such effects are poorly explained by a reading practice that has exactly one trick up its sleeve.

Second, the scholarly focus on the stereotype tends to flatten its textual objects to such an extent it almost always under-reads the complexities of even the most stereotypical texts. Consider as an example an episode of *Beulah* (ABC, 1950–53), in which black maid Beulah (Louise Beavers) has somehow gotten the (mistaken, but that pretty much goes without saying on *Beulah*) idea that her white employer, to whom she refers as "Miss Alice," is pregnant. She passes this "information" on to Alice's husband, "Mr. Harry," who promptly begins dreaming of the new arrival. As he and Beulah's boyfriend, the hapless handyman Bill, are hanging outdoor lanterns for a picnic, they exchange the following lines of dialogue:

> BILL: "Anything else you'd like me to hang up, Mr. HARRY?"
> HARRY: "A little boy with Donny's smile or a little girl with blonde curls."
> BILL: "Huh?"

While the bizarre allusion to lynching here, and to the lynching of a suburban white child at that, does nothing to mitigate the organizing racism of *Beulah* in general or this episode in particular, surely we can at least agree that something complicated is going on here. Is the text allowing itself to imagine, surreptitiously and fleetingly, deadly and racially coded violence against its own idealized whiteness? Regardless of how we read this moment, this is not the kind of textual detail likely to be spotted under the coarse lens of "the stereotype" or the "negative image."

Third, such analytical approaches under-read as well the complex relationships between texts deploying stereotypes and the televisual fields that surround them. Such fields, organized by flow, genre, and historical moment, or what Robert Deming has called "the viewer's television archives," may tend either to support or to challenge stereotypes.[7] Recall, for example, the first season of CBS's *Survivor*. *Survivor*, with its "tribes," "talismans," and "idols," is always organized by the most transparently racist and ethnocentric tropes; that first season, to boot, was populated by African Americans who either couldn't work (Ramona) or couldn't swim (Gervase), and by a winner (Richard) who, despite being gay, managed to market himself, through his unapologetic emphasis on "playing the game," as the perfect corporate white guy. But these effects were complicated, that summer, by the Reebok ads that punctuated the program throughout its run. Featuring two geeky, twentysomething white guys in *Survivor*-inspired situations, these ads ironized Richard's game-playing. Their characters played the game *badly*, continually and unnecessarily adopting the most extreme and foolhardy approaches to "surviving," only to have their stupidity pointed out to them by well-meaning (and Reebok-clad) passersby, usually women and/or persons of color. If another Richard, Richard Dyer, is correct that one of the constitutive and enduring tropes of whiteness is the white man's conquest of the wilderness, surely these ads serve a destabilizing and unpredictable function in relation to the text of *Survivor* "proper."[8]

Fourth, by taking what is only the most obvious form of televisual racism—the stereotype or "negative image"—as the medium's singular or even dominant form of racial ideology, stereotype-focused accounts risk drastically under-describing other problematic representational modalities in which racial types figure marginally, if at all. Such forms are more subtle and may be just as insidious. Consider (as I will throughout this book), for example, the long tradition, from Nat King Cole to André Braugher, of respectful—even deferential—depictions of the exemplary Negro, depictions whose positive effects for white hegemony may outweigh their effects among blacks as "positive images."[9] Consider as well the documentary gaze, from Edward R. Murrow's *Harvest of Shame* to Bill Moyers's *The Crisis in the Black Family*, which fetishizes "accuracy" while gaping ethnographically at its black Others.[10] And consider the consistent reduction of mass black politics, from the March on Washington to the Million Man March, to their implications for whites or their potential for "unrest."[11]

Fifth, and finally, prevailing descriptions of the relations between African Americans and television, like Dates and Barlow's, in which powerful white opinion leaders slander passive blacks, are inadequate to explain these modalities and the overdetermined industrial conditions and social relations that produce them. Because they rest on the assumption that racial stereotypes invented "as far back as the colonial era" have persisted pretty much unchanged, they rest as well on the denial that television, as an historically situated and technologically specific phenomenon, might both organize and be organized by similarly specific racial formations. These descriptions are inadequate, in other words, because they fail to recognize the ways in which African American persons, collectivities, and politics have collided at crucial moments in television history with industrial self-interest, cynicism, and even, on occasion, the desire to do the right thing, to produce not only the content of television's programs, but their form and reception as well. To put it more bluntly, these descriptions are inadequate because they fail to apprehend the extent to which progressive postwar racial politics and American television have nurtured, relied on, and exploited one another.

Let me give you an example.

ISSUES AND SOME ANSWERS

There are eight pieces of thirty-two-year-old correspondence in a file marked "American Broadcasting Company" among the papers of Martin Luther King, Jr., at the Archives of the Martin Luther King, Jr., Center for Nonviolent Social Change in Atlanta. The letters chronicle the attempts, starting late in 1967, by *Issues and Answers* producer Peggy Whedon to book King as a guest on her series. Prompted, apparently, by news of the upcoming Poor People's Campaign, Whedon wrote to King on December 5: "It has been far too long since you have been with us on ISSUES AND ANSWERS, and we would like to plan towards a program with you for the time in April when you start your plan of civil disobedience in Washington, D.C." Hoping to entice the ever-overscheduled King, Whedon promised that "ISSUES AND ANSWERS offers the ideal format and best TV time slot for a presentation by you to the American people."[12]

King's secretary at the Southern Christian Leadership Conference (SCLC), Dora McDonald, replied to Whedon on January 11, 1968: "Dr. King asked me to write to say that it will be possible for him to appear on *Issues and Answers* on Sunday, February 11, 1968. In keeping with the telephone conversation we had recently, he will not appear on any similar program at least thirty days before or after your engagement."[13] But King's schedule and the network's conflicted: ABC would preempt *Issues and Answers* on February 11 in favor of its telecast of the Winter Olympics from Grenoble. Could King, Whedon asked in her January 22 letter to McDonald, appear on Sunday, March 24?[14] No, McDonald replied, he was already scheduled to appear on *Face the Nation* that day.[15]

Undaunted, Whedon wrote back on February 13, again pitching the potential program's efficacy for both ABC and the civil rights cause:

> Since we cannot confirm a March date with Doctor King for a guest appearance on "Issues and Answers", I'd like to suggest a late April appearance after the Washington demonstrations. This would probably involve a summary of what had been accomplished and a look ahead to the summer.
>
> We shall wait to hear from you as to a good Sunday . . . , a Sunday that would have a strong impact on audiences and on news stories. Since the program is carried in every large city in the United States, let's find a Sunday that would be mutually effective and important. Would April 28th be a good date?[16]

April 28th was not a good date. Murdered on April 4th, King would be by then relegated posthumously to television genres other than Sunday afternoon public affairs programming: catastrophe coverage (news of the assassination and its aftermath), media event (the funeral), and, eventually, liberal documentary retrospective and public service announcement.[17]

I cite this correspondence here as evidence of the complex relations of power at work in the relationship between the industry and the movement. Note, for example, that Whedon approaches King, not the other way around. Note the frankness with which she pitches *Issues and Answers*—with its "ideal format," "best TV time slot," and address to "every large city in the United States"—as a publicity vehicle for the campaign. And note how her emphasis on the "mutuality" of interest between ABC's program and King's movement constitutes a near-admission that each will be using the other for particular kinds of gain: while King and the campaign will benefit from national exposure, ABC will get exclusive access to King, at least for thirty days, and "a strong impact on audiences and on news stories."

A darling of the press since the Montgomery Bus Boycott, King enjoyed media access that was unique among movement activists. In 1968 he would have been particularly sought after by television producers, despite his opposition the Vietnam War and his shift to the Left on economic issues, as a "moderate" with respect to race relations. But if King—as a "reasonable" black leader with immense telegenicity—constituted for people like Whedon the prize on which they always had their eyes, I would argue that this had as much to do with a historical alliance between television and the civil rights movement as with King's singular televisual luminosity. The first two chapters of this book chart the early years of this alliance, which emerges in the wake of the lynching of Emmett Till and continues at least until 1965.

There was much more connecting civil rights with television than the temporal coincidence between the rapid expansion of the southern movement and the similar growth in television's penetration and profits. One of the central arguments of *Black, White, and In Color* is that from 1955 to 1965, both the civil rights movement and the television industry shared the urgent desire to forge a new, and newly *national*, consensus on the meanings and functions of racial difference. For its part, the southern movement's most consistent and effective gesture against segregation was to contrast the racial terrorism of the South with national ideals and democratic discourses. At exactly the same moment, television was becoming a national medium. The continued expansion of the industry's profits thus depended on its ability to exploit in programming the visuality and topicality of race across sectional borders. This in turn required a newly *national* consensus on the range of race's possible meanings, one that could spare networks the ire of southern affiliates, who were, from the perspective of the New York-based corporations, out of step with the rest of the country with respect to racial representation. Television and the civil rights movement, then, through a perhaps unlikely coincidence of interests, formed powerful allies for each other during this period.

In my view, the intertwining of network and movement has enormous consequences for our understanding both of TV history and African American televisual representation. With respect to TV history, if the picture I paint in the first and second chapters is an accurate one, then many of telejournalism's conventions and procedures were established in crucial relation to the various imperatives to represent African American persons, collectivities, and political struggles at work during the period. In other words, if the conventions adopted in the early years of television news were organized to a great extent by the genre's encounter with the movement, and if news departments were crucial to the networks' self-understandings, then we find race squarely at the center of affiliate relations, industrial institution-building, and generic formation. If television historians of the late 1950s and early 1960s were really to take this fact on board, our understanding of the period would in my view shift both enormously and unpredictably.

With respect to black televisuality, to claim that televisual racial representation in information genres was dominated by images of the civil rights movement in the late '50s and early '60s is not to claim that stereotypical representation in other genres was eradicated or even came temporarily to a screeching halt during the period. It is rather to note that such representation existed alongside representations of many of the most forceful and articulate African Americans that the nation has known, and to suggest that these sets of representations might fruitfully be read *in relation to* one another.[18] It is to propose, in other words, that it is in the generic interplay between "information" and "entertainment," that something like *Amos 'n' Andy* (produced in 1951–53, but widely available in syndication until 1966) can be understood.

The first two chapters of *Black, White, and In Color* offer interrelated arguments in support of my claims for movement/network cooperation during the years from 1955 to 1965. Chapter 1, " 'In a crisis we must have a sense of drama': Civil Rights and Televisual Information," considers the relationship between television information programming and the Southern civil rights movement, especially SCLC and the pre–black power Student Nonviolent Coordinating Committee (SNCC). Drawing upon archival documents, histories of journalism and of the movement, and the memoirs of both journalists and television information workers, I examine first what the movement meant to telejournalists and then what telejournalists meant for the movement, unraveling the knot of overlapping and common interest in which each was joined to the other.

In the second chapter, "The Double Life of 'Sit-In,' " I recapitulate the movement described in the first, pursuing similar questions by focusing on a single text. Because the NBC documentary "Sit-In," which aired December 20, 1960, came at the beginning of a "boom" in network documentary production, it has much to teach us about what network news organizations hoped to accomplish with such films. Through close reading of the documentary's narrative structure and deployment of the figure of Chet Huntley, I argue that civil rights representation like "Sit-In" was an important mechanism for establishing the objective *gravitas* of telejournalism at an early moment in its history, even as the documentary was at pains to present the gains of the Nashville movement as inevitable. In the second part of the chapter, I discuss the movement's use of "Sit-In" during the early 1960s as a recruitment and training film in civil disobedience. Since "Sit-In" was an important text within the civil rights movement, it affords us some insight into the reception practices that greeted civil rights representation among progressive blacks.

Coverage of the events at Little Rock, Birmingham, and Selma are clearly the most important texts of civil rights television for both the medium and the movement. As many have argued (more on this in chapter 1), Little Rock granted television news a new seriousness, which was deepened in the coverage of Birmingham and Selma. And there is wide consensus that Birmingham and Selma contributed considerably to the passage of the Civil Rights Act and the Voting Rights act, respectively. These televisual moments are linked not just by the power of their impact, but also by a specific element of their content: the intersection of African American bodies and the violent tactics of southern police. Central to the movement strategy of calling southern institutions to account for racism in full view of the entire nation was the historically slippery relation between official and unofficial enforcement of Jim Crow. As any serious history of the Ku Klux Klan will establish, the official agents of the state charged with maintaining segregation had, since Reconstruction, been closely allied with white racial terrorists of the unofficial kind; many were themselves Klan members.[19] The quite-reliable tendency of southern police to privilege local custom over federal law both fascinated and appalled northern news workers; their film became visible evidence for the movement in its case against the South. In this respect, the first two chapters of *Black, White, and In Color* constitute the first half of a diptych representing two moments in the recent history of relations among television, blacks, and law enforcement: 1955–1965 and the 1990s. As a diptych, the book as a whole interrogates the shifting relations of televised law enforcement to conservative racial projects.

TELEVISION AND CONSERVATIVE RACIAL PROJECTS AFTER THE '60s

Black, White, and In Color treats both race and policing as phenomena that change over time. It is interested both in certain thematic, generic, and representational holdovers from the first moment it treats to the second, and in the historical specificity of those moments. Here I will propose an account of the specificities of the second, paying particular, albeit brief, attention to the reconstitution of conservative racial ideology and practices in the wake of the civil rights era, and the centrality of television to their institutionalization during the Reagan-Bush years.

A full exposition of the history of racial politics and meanings for the past thirty-odd years is obviously beyond the scope of this book. But it is worth summarizing briefly the major forms that reaction against African American civil rights gains has taken during this period. First, I should note that at least one of these gains has not been overturned: it is no longer possible, in mainstream American national culture, to appear to be against racial equality. As Michael Omi and Howard Winant write, "In the aftermath of the 1960s, any effective challenge to the egalitarian ideals framed by the minority movements could no longer rely on the racism of the past. Racial equality had to be acknowledged as a desirable goal."[20] Television scholar Herman Gray concurs: "Even when blackness functioned as the chief icon against which conservative Republicans ran for political office, it was important for them not to appear racist."[21] So the politics of racial reaction are first and foremost a politics of euphemism and recoding. We might think of Nixon's call to "law and order" on behalf of an (implicitly white) "silent majority" as an inaugural example of such euphemism in the post–civil rights era.[22]

Since the mid-1970s, these new right and neoconservative recodings have been organized around a central reversal: the doctrine that, in Kimberlé Crenshaw's words, "singles out race-specific civil rights policies as one of the most significant threats to the democratic political system." She goes on:

> Emphasizing the need for strictly color-blind policies, this view calls for the repeal of affirmative action and other race-specific remedial policies, urges an end to class-based remedies, and calls for the administration to limit remedies to what it calls "actual victims" of discrimination.[23]

By calling race consciousness per se antidemocratic, the Right accomplished several tasks at once. First, this discursive shift supported one of their most important objectives: to stop in its tracks the long-term efforts of the legal arm of the NAACP to seek meaningful legal equality for African Americans through the courts.[24] Conservative legal scholars used their equation of color-blindness with democracy to urge the courts to emphasize "equality of process" for blacks—rather than "equality of result," as the NAACP had tried to do. Briefly, "equality of result" seeks to end African American subordination and asks the courts to serve the national interest by eliminating its effects. "Equality of process," on the other hand, envisions such subordination as isolated acts against individuals and "seeks," in Crenshaw's words, "to proscribe only certain kinds of subordinating acts, and then only when other interests are not overburdened." Conservative arguments against "equality of result" proved effective at hobbling racial minorities as they sought legal redress for discrimination.[25]

In addition, figuring race consciousness as a threat to democracy helped the Right to disseminate the notion of "reverse discrimination" by people of color against law-abiding middle-class white male taxpayers. The notion of "reverse discrimination, in turn, helped conservatives render discursively acceptable their systematic attacks both on people of color and the poor, who were now redefined, post–"War on

Poverty," as a national problem of a different sort. The poor in general and the black poor in particular were now, in Herman Gray's words, "distinguished by sedation and satisfaction of bodily pleasures, dependency, immorality, hostility, erosion of standards, loss of civic responsibility, and lack of respect for traditional values," and thus as "undeserving" of national concern.[26] Their demands, and those of their "liberal" allies, on the welfare state were now depicted as greedy and illegitimate claims to too-large slices of a shrinking national pie to which white taxpayers had too little access.

Finally, the Right's attack on race-conscious social policies allowed it to reposition whiteness as victim rather than victimizer. And, like the notion of "reverse discrimination," this move managed, according to Gray, "to take away from blacks the moral authority . . . won in the civil rights movement."[27] As I argue in chapter 1, it was precisely the moral authority of the movement that provided the underpinning for its alliance with television, insofar as this authority was made manifest by "bearing the cross" both of racial injustice and of what José Muñoz has called "the burden of liveness." In the context of the southern civil rights movement, bearing "the burden of liveness" required movement workers to produce arresting televisual images juxtaposing peaceful protest with physical suffering at the hands of violent segregationists.[28] Given this representational history, which so dramatically supported the equation of whiteness with vicious self-interest, the conservative effort to displace moral authority with respect to racial justice from blacks to whites required new kinds of televised racial representation.

The chief mechanism for this displacement during the 1980s was television news. If, as Gray argues convincingly, "blackness was constructed along a continuum ranging from menace on one end to immorality on the other, with irresponsibility located somewhere in the middle," this trope was disseminated through a nightly representational flood of "black male gang members, black male criminality, crumbling black families, black welfare cheats, black female crack users, and black teen pregnancy."[29] He sums up this process this way:

> Throughout the Reagan/Bush 1980s, commercial network television news programs brought us more and more people, mostly blacks and latinos, who seemed beyond the reasonable comprehension of [the] popular common sense of public and civic responsibility, except as deviants, dependents and threats. If television news was to be believed, these mostly black and brown people seemed to commit more crime, have more babies, use more drugs, and be more incompetent with respect to individual and civic responsibility.[30]

Television news in the 1980s, then, participated actively in the new construction of black criminality, addiction, and irresponsibility.[31] In the process, it helped undergird a national shift in the understanding of blackness that certainly eased the accomplishment of the Reaganite racial agenda at the level of public policy and discourse. And these shifts toward a more conservative understanding of racial movements has been remarkably durable. It is the second major argument of this book that 1990s television representing law and criminality proved eerily effective at continuing the criminalization of blackness that was the central racial project of television news of the '80s.[32]

"Law and order" programming of the 1990s, then, is the other picture in *Black, White, and In Color*'s diptych examining race and policing. During the civil rights years, the alliance between news workers and the movement produced a particular set of coded identifications linking disparate televisual information texts: television asked its viewers, black and white, to identify *with* nonviolent black protest and *against* the violent representatives of the southern state. By the early 1990s, though, television was asking its viewers to perform identifications that are precisely the opposite of those we find in the earlier period, to identify *against* blacks, who are now generally associated with criminality, and *with* the state power of the police. This dramatic shift suggests not only the durability of post–civil rights era conservatism with respect to race, but also the necessity that those on the Left refocus our attention on policing as one of the most important ways in which racial struggle is now being waged. Indeed, the excesses of contemporary policing in U.S. urban centers seem increasingly to be where the incompleteness of the American civil rights project is most visible. It is certainly ironic that the movement's highly publicized and strategically successful encounters with Southern law enforcement personalities like Birmingham's Bull Connor and Selma's Jim Clark — encounters explicitly staged for television — have yielded in the contemporary moment to contests with police racism and corruption that seem to have little if any political efficacy, and that are merely fodder for television's docudramatic fictionalization. It's my hope that the juxtaposition of circumstances, representations, and arguments in the two parts of this book will suggest why we need so badly, right now, to wrench our public discussions of policing out of the realm of televised fiction.

Chapters 3 and 4 interrogate the widespread tendency for "liveness" or its traces to serve as a sign of televisual blackness. In chapter 1, I establish the contexts for some of the informational tropes of liveness or quasi-liveness that come to dominate civil rights representation's mediation of African American persons, politics, and collectivities. It is the latter-day versions of these tropes — the persistent association of what Phillip Brian Harper has called "mimetic realism" with black subjects and their representation — that mobilize the depictions I discuss in the book's second half.[33]

In chapter 3, I read a group of texts, each treating in some form the beating of Rodney King by LAPD officers and its aftermath. I examine how "liveness," which Jane Feuer and others have identified as the organizing ideology of television, served also as the ideology organizing the public understanding of the historical events comprising the beating and what followed.[34] Through a reading of *L.A. Law* and *Doogie Howser, M.D.*'s treatment of the uprisings following the Simi Valley verdict, I trace how fictional televisual forms appropriate liveness for their own purposes, thus representing (perhaps inadvertently) a struggle among televisual forms to represent the nation. And I consider how race figures into network television's self-understanding during this period.

In chapter 4, I examine *Brooklyn South*'s versions of the torture of Abner Louima. If chapter 3 focuses chiefly on how collisions between police brutality and televisual representation force revisions to the medium's understanding of its social functions, economic viability, and forms of address, here I am concerned with the question of how cultural representation can aid in the project of abridging civil rights. Against the backdrop of "Giuliani Time," the mayoral administration of Rudolph Giuliani, I ask whether the cop show, as a genre, can ease the implementation of a political program of "law and order" that is broadly racist and classist in its effects.

Chapter 5 serves as a kind of conclusion to *Black, White, and In Color*. Here I try to pull back from the specific texts and historical contexts encountered in earlier chapters to consider the relation between television and African American political and social aspiration more broadly. In particular, I consider the usefulness of the widespread tendency, among African American cultural and political leaders, to equate access to television with access to power. I hope to trouble this equation by noting that television's "positive images" of black "civil rights subjects" are always paired with, and thus counteracted by, negative ones, which I call the subject of civil rights undone: that television representation for blacks, and particularly for black men, has a troubling tendency to slide into forms of surveillance or ethnography; and that the historical inaccessibility of television as a space for black women's self-representation severely undermines the medium's potential as a vehicle for black political possibility.

"In a crisis we must have a sense of drama": Civil Rights and Televisual Information

THE BURDEN OF LIVENESS

RATHER than locating the dominating tropes of African American televisual representation in a set of stock characters or "stereotypes," in this chapter I look instead to the historical relationship between African American political struggles and televisual institutions and, more particularly to a particular historical coincidence: the simultaneous rise of the southern civil rights movement in the wake of the Montgomery Bus Boycott, and of television news as an authoritative force in American public life. To complicate the now-dominant historical understanding that TV borrowed its tropes of blackness from a variety of representational sites all more or less indebted to the traditions of minstrelsy, I will argue that the period roughly from 1955 to 1965 was a crucial moment in the establishment of extremely durable ideological, rhetorical, and institutional procedures for the depiction of African American persons and politics on television, and that these procedures had less to do with black social subservience than with an emergent black political agency. For, as I have suggested in the introduction, American television has — and always has had — a liberal tradition of African American representation, and it is the representations comprising that tradition that are my central focus. One of the stock elements of such representations has been a certain documentary or ethnographic impulse, an imperative to "authenticity" in depictions of African Americans. Television's concern with "realism" in such representations has been at least as durable as its tendency to create black subjects out of whole cloth.

At least as durable, and perhaps also as dangerous: José Muñoz has called the imperative that people of color ceaselessly perform our own authenticity "the burden of liveness."[1] Noting that "the minoritarian subject is always encouraged to perform, *especially* when human and civil rights disintegrate," Muñoz further elaborates "the burden of liveness" as the "mandate to 'perform' for the amusement of the dominant power bloc." In other words, Muñoz collates the widely shared Western tendency to privilege live over recorded performance with a fetishizing racist or imperial gaze on bodies of color.

Thus Muñoz turns the more usual use of the term "liveness"—to describe a representational mode specific to television—on its head in productive ways. For both television scholars and for the medium itself, liveness has generally referred to the fact of television's capacity to transmit images more or less in real time (as opposed to film, which must be developed in order to signify). Among television scholars, live-ness refers as well to the corresponding and specious assertion that television representation has a privileged claim to immediacy and trans-parency.[2] Television's claim to be "live" has been central to its self-promotion and reception since its beginnings. But the medium's relation to its own liveness is a fraught one; indeed, television's constant and anxious insistence on its own liveness can only betray its fear of becom-ing technologically or culturally dead. Muñoz's notion of the "burden of liveness" suggests that it's not enough for television to *be* live: the medium needs as well to represent "authentic" persons of color, stock-piling *their* liveness to be borrowed back in times of political or repre-sentational crisis.

The "burden of liveness" as a "mandate" to perform for "the amuse-ment of the dominant power bloc"—amusement, yes, but also horror. For television's African American spectacles have persistently been char-acterized not only by black performance as "entertainment" but also as "information," to employ one of the medium's own favorite binaries. And black performances in information genres have most often been deployed, by African Americans themselves as well as by both cynical and well-meaning whites, to product outrage, trepidation, and alarm.

Part of my project here is to speculate on the underpinnings of the tendency for certain kinds of informational liveness to infiltrate even contemporary entertainment genres featuring black performance; such infiltration will be my object in chapter 3. For now, though, it suffices to say that the persistence of burdensome liveness as a structuring element of African American televisual representation has been produced not only by the medium's obsessive, anxious, and incessant claims to be (a)live, but also by specific historical circumstances arising in the 1950s that produced a set of lived practices of journalism and publicity. These practices coimplicated the movement and television information work-ers in a set of overlapping and common interests. In this respect, Muñoz's characterization of liveness as a "burden" evokes both Martin Luther King's understanding of the project of the civil rights move-ment—to persuade blacks to embrace the redemptive promise of suffer-ing on their own behalf and on that of future generations—and his customary figuration of that project in terms of bearing a burden, usu-ally a cross.[3] Taking up the burden of liveness—of producing televisual immediacy via black performances of physical suffering and political demand — was a primary focus of the movement and a crucial key to its success.

"PICTURES ARE THE POINT OF TELEVISION NEWS"

The civil rights movement played a crucial role in the emerging production practices and self-understanding of network information workers — the makers of news, documentary, and public affairs programming — during the 1950s. The fates of the movement and information genres in their formative periods were intertwined with each other not merely by temporal coincidence, or by what J. Fred MacDonald has called "the simultaneous emergence of the civil rights movement and television."[4] This convergence resulted also from a quite specific, if also quite fortuitous, collation of needs and resources. Telejournalism, obviously, needed vivid pictures and clear-cut stories; less obviously, it also sought political and cultural *gravitas*. For its part, the civil rights movement staked the moral authority of Christian nonviolence and the rhetoric of American democracy to make a new national culture; to succeed, it needed to have its picture taken and its stories told.

Although few take civil rights coverage as their explicit subject, the memoirs of television information workers who began their careers in the medium's early days provide clues to how the movement was understood within the emerging culture of telejournalism.[5] For example, former NBC News president Reuven Frank's memoir, *Out of Thin Air: The Brief Wonderful Life of Network News*, situates civil rights as the domestic issue on which NBC News cut its teeth.[6] "Television news began," he writes, in the book's inaugural sentence, "with the 1948 political conventions."[7] And the 1948 political conventions made interesting coverage, Frank claims, largely because of the battle among the Democrats over the party's civil rights plank. Here is Frank's description of that battle, quoted at some length:

> The party platform, the heart of the fight that was tearing the Democratic party apart, was scheduled for presentation Tuesday, the next day. For the first time in its young life, television would be present at a watershed event in history. The party's factions could not agree on a compromise position on civil rights, and the presentation of the platform was delayed all day. All day Tuesday and all that night, the arguing, the conciliating, the posturing, and the dealing continued. . . .

Then the television audience saw a historical event unfold spontaneously before its eyes, two days of conflict and resolution that changed the course of the country, the struggle to commit one of America's major parties to redress by law the disabilities that enshackled Negro Americans. In one form or another, the issue was to dominate American society for the rest of the century, but never was the issue so clear as it was at that convention, or seen so clearly as by the people who saw it covered live on television.[8]

I am less interested in the evident falsity of Frank's claims about the capacity of live television to impart "clarity" on "the issue" than I am in the fact that he makes them at all. Civil rights serves in this passage as television news's origin(al) story: "For the first time in its young life, television would be present at a watershed event in history," "the struggle to commit one of America's major parties to redress by law the disabilities that enshackled Negro Americans."[9] Here and elsewhere in the book, Frank situates television as the medium best suited to cover civil rights, and situates civil rights as a particularly apt story for television news. These reciprocal claims, I think, rely on what Frank understands to be the unique contribution of television journalism—its visuality. "Pictures," he insists, "*are* the point of television news."[10] The putative hypervisibility of racial difference—and racial violence as well—grants race privileged status in Frank's account of why television news "mattered more" than print journalism.[11] Frank elucidates these links in his description of a package on "the country's most important segregationist," Mississippi Senator James Eastland, which he produced for the NBC news program *Outlook*:

> [Eastland] was asked about repressive practices against Negroes in his state and his hometown. He indignantly rejected the imputation as incredible, because it would be illegal, a crime. He paused, then slowly and more quietly he said, "That is, if you could get the grand jury to indict."
>
> He pronounced it "indaht" and we let it hang there. He smiled. His round face beamed and his wire-rimmed spectacles shone as the smile persisted. It was another of those small occasions that justify the existence of television. Eastland clearly knew what he was saying; he was playing games with us. In a newspaper report, the smile would not have been visible, and he knew that. But like so many in those days, even politicians, he had yet to learn about television. So he smiled as he said it. Inferring smugness or hypocrisy from that smile in a newspaper account would have been considered bad journalism. We could have cut the film at Eastland's last word, as though his words mattered but how he said them did not. Television news people who have no feel for television, in time the majority, would have done it that way. On television, we were able to follow his last word with a few milliseconds of

smile, because pictures differ from words, and how they differ is not in degree but in kind.[12]

This passage's repetitions of the word "smile" indicate a certain self-aware strain here, marking its incapacity to describe adequately that which "a few milliseconds" of television can signify with ease: the smug performance of a sectionally marked whiteness, its corruption and privilege, its ill-conceived excess. Thus Frank's description of this moment clarifies the necessity of the imbrication of television with race trouble: on one hand, race and racial conflict fed the new medium's enormous appetite for visual spectacle; on the other, the mere fact of television's coverage served paradoxically to render racism visible in new ways, and to new audiences. But if Frank provides an account of why television covered the movement, the question of why television generally covered the movement *sympathetically* remains to be answered.

As Michael Curtin has observed, and as I shall discuss further in chapter 2, early television journalists often looked to the storytelling conventions of Hollywood, slotting televisual information into recognizable entertainment genres to garner audiences.[13] Like the reporting of the Cold War—the other big story of the fifties—coverage of the civil rights movement often played like the westerns on offer in the cinemas of the period, in which the distinctions between good and evil were sharply drawn. To put it another way, reporters in the South often ignored the journalistic imperative to neutrality. This can be attributed in part to the moral authority commanded by movement participants, who acted with remarkable courage in the face of the violent reprisals and economic deprivations that accompanied their activism. As movement stalwart John Lewis observes, the journalists covering Mississippi in 1964

> tried to remain objective, but there was no question that . . . [they] became very sympathetic to the movement. They couldn't help it. Day in and day out, going into those backwoods communities as well as to the more visible towns and cities of that state, watching people singing and praying from the bottoms of their souls, seeing the sorts of conditions these people were living in, with nothing for a front step but an old metal bucket turned upside down, with front porches that were nothing but a couple of planks nailed over dirt and mud, with no plumbing or electricity or decent clothes for their children or themselves, just pure and utter poverty—these reporters *had* to be moved.[14]

The accretion of detail in Lewis's last, long sentence here begins to suggest something of how the process he describes worked in practice: constant exposure to the everyday life of the movement won the press over.

The press's widespread abandonment of "balance" can be attributed as well to the self-evident bankruptcy of the segregationist position, motivated as it was by brutal and obvious self-interest on one hand and irrational hatred on the other. The assessment of Paul Good, who covered the 1964 movement in Saint Augustine for ABC news, is typical:

> Reporters are supposed to revere objectivity. . . . I tried to tell both sides as far as there were sides to tell. But how would you report a Dachau or a Buchenwald? By faithfully expounding Hitler's thesis of the Jewish problem, so much space for the international conspiracy of World Zionism, so much for descriptions of mothers leading children into gas chambers? . . . The contrast was not so extreme in Saint Augustine, unless inhumanity to man is everywhere and always the same degree of mortal sin, but it was vivid enough.[15]

The difficulties Good describes here were compounded by the fact that segregationists were unable to articulate their position to journalists in ways that would gain the sympathies of audiences outside the South; their arguments about states' rights, which were perhaps their best hope rhetorically, were so transparently euphemistic for their underlying fears of lost political power that they rung false virtually from the moment *Brown v. Board of Education* was handed down. Faced with a public relations crisis of ever-increasing proportions, many segregationists blamed press coverage for "the South's problem with the Negro," and many chose to counter their bad press with intimidation of and violence against reporters.[16] Faced with bat-wielding, camera-smashing segregationists advocating the perpetuation of American apartheid on one side and with nonviolent civil rights workers seeking to redeem the promises of American democracy on the other, it is not particularly surprising that journalists tended to empathize with the latter.

   Howard K. Smith's memoir, *Events Leading up to My Death*, provides an extended meditation on the question of objectivity in coverage of the movement. In 1961, Smith and his crew went south to shoot the CBS documentary "Who Speaks for Birmingham?" Before they left, Smith's producer, David Lowe, issued a warning that seems to self-destruct on utterance. As Smith represents this moment, "Lowe summed up our mission, 'You know how this report is going to turn out. However balanced we try to keep it, the Establishment is going to look awful because its position is awful. So we have to work harder than ever to give it *a form of balance*.'"[17] This imperative, however half-hearted, to "balance" became even more difficult to realize when Smith and his crew, tipped off by a publicity-hungry Klan leader, found themselves at Birmingham's bus terminal the day the first Freedom Riders arrived. Smith and his cameras witnessed a melee carefully planned by Birmingham Police Commissioner, Bull Connor, in concert with local Klansmen, in which

> the riders were being dragged from the bus to the station. In a corridor I entered they were being beaten with bicycle chains and blackjacks and steel knucks. When they fell they were kicked mercilessly, the scrotum being the favored target, and pounded with baseball bats.[18]

Ultimately, the "form of balance" Lowe and Smith gave "Who Speaks for Birmingham" — which ended with Smith calling on President Kennedy to "restate" the laws of the land to recalcitrant southerners — got Smith fired from CBS in a conflict with William Paley over the meaning, precisely, of "balance." ("The Civil Rights issue was not one over which reasonable minds might differ," Smith later wrote.[19]) But I would argue that Smith's dismissal merely imposed a limit on what was already standard operating procedure with respect to the treatment of civil rights by television journalism, rather than ruling it out of court. This suggestion is borne out by the fact that Smith was almost immediately hired by ABC, where he continued to advocate for SCLC-style civil rights throughout the 1960s.[20]

If television journalists risked the authority generally accruing to "balance," this gesture must be read as the product not only of the contingencies of the movement, but also as a self-interested one, both for news organizations and for the networks of which they were a part. For news workers, civil rights reporting promised — and delivered — precisely the cultural capital the new medium needed. Because publicity was such a crucial part of the movement's strategies, and because public opinion was such an important element in the disposition of particular civil rights struggles, coverage of the movement allowed network news not only to report, but also to intervene in, national culture and political discourse. The networks' response to the 1957 integration crisis in Little Rock is an important case in point.

Taylor Branch has called the events in Little Rock "the first on-site news extravaganza of the modern television era" and indeed Little Rock was the perfect story for network news.[21] It was oversaturated with dramatic images, and it satisfied television's craving for moral absolutes. On September 4, for example, the day Arkansas governor Orval Faubus ordered the National Guard to bar nine black students from entering Central High School, viewers witnessed the mob's rage, its violence (including, famously, the attack on black journalist Alex Wilson, who was beaten with a brick on camera), and in stark contrast, the almost uncanny composure of Elizabeth Eckford, one of the black students, who had gotten separated from the others and had to walk alone through a mass of threatening whites. And on September 25, after Eisenhower reluctantly sent units of the 101st Airborne Division to Little Rock to protect the students, viewers watched the "Little Rock Nine"—linked visually with federal authority and the rule of law—walking into school surrounded by soldiers armed with fixed bayonets.

Little Rock was not only the right story for television news; it was the right story at the right time. The crisis materialized as the regionally uneven distribution of affiliates and television households (more on which to follow) was subsiding, and as television's penetration into American homes was almost complete. As Thomas Leonard has pointed out, "Little Rock's troubles reached a viewing public that dwarfed the television audience when the ['50s] began: eighty-five percent of all homes were watching for five hours a day."[22] Thus a large and newly national audience followed the story intently, and coverage was unrelenting: NBC led with John Chancellor's reports from Arkansas every night for a month.[23] As one journalist put it, the collective nightly ritual came to resemble "a national evening séance."[24] For the networks, that séance conjured new legitimacy and influence for television news, affording them restored prestige as it afforded their news divisions political clout: by framing the story as they did, reporters not only helped to forge, but also participated in, the public opinion that eventually forced Ike's hand.

With so much at stake in network reportage, it is not surprising that the civil rights beat was a highly desirable one among reporters, and it is no accident that covering the movement made the reputations of many of the major figures of television journalism—including John Chancellor, Peter Jennings, Dan Rather, Harry Reasoner, Howard K. Smith, Sander Vanocur, and Mike Wallace. But the stakes in civil rights coverage were high as well in network precincts other than the news division, for the profitability of the networks required the elaboration of a new national consensus on race.

"WE HAVE SHUT OURSELVES OFF FROM THE REST OF THE WORLD"

While TV always aspired to a national address, the early expansion of television, with respect to the numbers both of television stations and of homes with television sets, was very uneven across the country. The medium grew most rapidly in the Northeast and most slowly in the deep South.[25] This uneven development was exacerbated by the FCC's freeze on the licensing of new stations from 1948 to 1952, while it tried to resolve a number of technical issues having to do with channel separation and the UHF band.[26] The freeze left Arkansas, Mississippi, and South Carolina completely without television at least until 1953.[27]

The unevenness of television's national penetration had crucial implications for network/affiliate relations during the second half of the 1950s. During this period, the completion of coaxial cable and relay links to the networks marked the full incorporation of southern affiliates into the networks; in addition the South offered a growth market for programmers and advertisers, as southern viewership continued to grow after the rest of the country had been saturated with both stations and sets. At the same time, to complicate matters further, network/affiliate relations were under considerable governmental and regulatory scrutiny. As the number of television stations increased after the freeze, station owners, many of whom had been located in one- or two-station markets and were thus able to affiliate with more than one network, lost much of their bargaining power in negotiating with the networks, particularly NBC and CBS. At issue were station compensation fees (the station's share of advertising revenues from the network's sale of time in the local market) and option time (network access to affiliate airtime). Option time served to guarantee that the networks would have high "clearance" rates, or, in other words, that a high percentage of affiliates would broadcast, or "clear," network programming, thus allowing the networks to charge the highest possible rates for advertising. Concerned about antitrust issues, a number of congressional committees spent considerable effort during the second half of the 1950s studying the question of whether option time was analogous to the block booking that had been outlawed by the Paramount decision. Though the FCC ultimately declined to address option time during the 1950s, these hearings served to keep the imperative to high clearance rates firmly in the networks' view.[28]

By the late '50s, the economic and regulatory climate combined with the political climate in the South to produce a quandary for the industry. For a number of reasons, it was in the networks' interest to strengthen ties to their southern affiliates during this period, but the percolating race trouble in the South threatened those ties. More specifically, disparate sectional assumptions about what counted as acceptable racial representation on television produced conflicts between the networks—northern both in location and temperament—and their southern affiliates. These disparities had been submerged during television's early years: when audiences were concentrated in the Northeast, programmers could afford to be somewhat experimental in their deployment of black performance in both entertainment and information genres.[29] White southern audiences, however, were likely to balk at black performance in *any* genre, and this tendency—which in some cases grew as the civil rights movement continued—threatened clearance rates. The industry made certain concessions with respect to entertainment programming: *The Nat King Cole Show* was cancelled in 1957 when it failed to garner a national sponsor due to advertisers' reluctance to "offend" southern audiences, and CBS served up the remarkable series *The Gray Ghost*, about a heroic confederate general, just as the battle of Little Rock was raging.[30] But, for the reasons I've suggested, the stakes with respect to information programming were too high for the networks to concede to southern tastes. As the civil rights movement was enticing television information workers, many southern affiliates were systematically refusing to clear news and documentaries about civil rights produced by the networks.

On a May 26, 1963 episode of Howard K. Smith's *News and Comment*, black Birmingham attorney Charles Morgan discussed this policy with respect to network documentaries:

> [Birmingham] is a city where for any number of years we have shut ourselves off from the rest of the world. . . . For instance . . . I believe "Walk in My Shoes" was a program produced by ABC. But the people here [in Birmingham] didn't see "Walk in My Shoes" because locally the television station didn't want to show it to them. They didn't see "Who Speaks for the South." They didn't see the *NBC White Paper* on the sit-ins.[31]

Morgan's assertions are borne out by television historian Steven Classen's research on one of the local stations in Jackson, Mississippi, WLBT. Classen notes that "in Jackson, [the] mediated omission of African American images and perspectives was nearly complete . . . and extended well into the sixties."[32] He elaborates:

> [T]he station staff was careful not only regarding what to include, but also what to exclude from the schedule—most notably programming that showcased articulate African Americans, such as NBC's *Nat King Cole Show*, or offerings that explicitly addressed southern race relations. For example, of the seven regularly scheduled NBC network "public affairs" programs that occasionally discussed racial integration and were offered to affiliates during approximately fourteen months between 1962 and 1963, WLBT chose to regularly air only the *Today Show*, and even then allegedly omitted "pro-integrationist" portions of that program (86).

While WLBT is an infamous case—African American activism against the station's persistently racist practices prevented its relicensing in 1969—the kinds of practices Classen describes here were widespread among southern affiliates, whose managers often viewed network-produced racial representation as integrationist propaganda. Anti-network sentiment ran high in many precincts: John Chancellor recalls that the networks were known, in some quarters at least, as "the Nigger Broadcasting Company (NBC), the Communist Broadcasting System (CBS) or the Asshole Broadcasting Company (ABC)."[33]

In the late 1950s and early 1960s, then, the television industry was faced with a number of competing factors constraining the representation of African Americans, their culture, and their political struggles. On one hand, the civil rights movement served network news organizations well in the various ways I've described; on the other, some southern affiliates threatened clearance rates by refusing to air network news viewed by southern station managers as critical of segregation. On one hand, television wanted to exploit the visuality and topicality of race trouble in both news and entertainment programming; on the other, network bosses wanted to avoid alienating southern audiences and provoking southern affiliates.[34] At the heart of these conflicts were sectionally specific understandings of the meanings and functions of race; these specificities threatened television's self-constitution as a properly national form addressing an audience assumed to share certain core ideological assumptions about the privileges of citizenship and the rule of law, and thus threatened the profits to be garnered from selling such an audience to advertisers. In this regard, the networks shared common cause with the movement, which sought to produce precisely such a national consensus. No wonder, then, that network programming tended to ease the achievement of movement goals.

"THAT CYCLE OF VIOLENCE AND PUBLICITY"

For their part, the key organizations of the southern civil rights movement — the Southern Christian Leadership Conference (SCLC), the Congress of Racial Equality (CORE), and the Student Nonviolent Coordinating Committee (SNCC) — all understood the importance of television in placing southern violence and intransigence on the national agenda, though each group's media-relations strategies were slightly different. Generally, nationally broadcast television news served the movement in two crucial if contradictory ways: on one hand, it tended to modulate segregationist violence against civil rights workers in the field; on the other, it captured and amplified the violence that movement demonstrations occasionally sought, replacing it within a national, rather than regional, context, in which it carried very different meanings.[35]

Television cameras provided a kind of safety net for those in the movement, who mention them frequently in oral histories and movement memoirs. Ruby Hurley, for example, the veteran Birmingham activist who opened the first NAACP office in the deep South, observes that "to me the fifties were much worse than the sixties. When I was out there by myself, for instance, there were no TV cameras with me to give me any protection. There were no reporters traveling with me to give me protection, because when the eye of the press or the eye of the camera was on the situation, it was different."[36] Andrew Young recalls objecting to SNCC's plans for Freedom Summer; in his view the project was recklessly dangerous, because "the presence of national media was virtually the only inhibitor of official violence, and you simply could not get that kind of attention for people in dozens of towns in Mississippi."[37] Albert Turner, commenting on why the 1965 demonstration in Marion, Alabama, became so violent, claims that

> one of the major reasons that thing was so bad that night, they shot the [cameramen's] lights out, and nobody was able to report what really happened. They turned all the lights out, shot the lights out, and they beat people at random. They didn't have to be marching. All you had to do was be black. And they hospitaled fifteen or twenty folks. And they just was intending to kill someone as an example, and they did kill Jimmie Jackson.[38]

Willie Bolden, an SCLC worker who was also in Marion, notes that "in filming, in many cases, they missed a lot of it because if the shit was gonna *really* go down, those folk tried to get those cameras out of the way first. And many times even after they were able to put the camera back into motion, much of the real *bloody* part of these marches was all over."[39]

These comments point out the doubleness of the effects that cameras could have on the day-to-day life of the movement. Their presence afforded movement workers a measure of protection against their segregationist opposition by signaling the capacity to broadcast southern race trouble nationally, to an audience unschooled in the traditional regional interpretations of racial terrorism. But, as I've suggested, cameras also tended in themselves to aggravate racist rage and violence, precisely by marking the extent to which the perpetuation of southern race relations was increasingly out of southern hands. The result was a delicate balance between provocation and restraint that was difficult for movement leaders to control precisely. Journalists and civil rights historians agree, though, that achieving and wielding such control was an explicit aim of SCLC: as Adam Fairclough argues in his history of the organization, "By carefully selecting its targets, SCLC . . . publicized white repression to its fullest possible effect. It contrived to do this, moreover, while keeping white violence to a minimum: SCLC's very presence, accompanied as it was by a phalanx of reporters and cameramen, inhibited white officials and restrained them in their use of violence."[40]

In the rest of this section I will discuss SCLC's media strategy, drawing from archival sources, movement memoirs, and critical studies of the organization. Narrowing the focus to SCLC inevitably produces some distortions, the most important of which is the risk of reproducing mainstream media's own obsession with King and their tendency to cover him to the exclusion of other movement leaders. And, given that the SCLC media strategy always concentrated on major media outlets, my observations here will certainly obscure strategies like SNCC's, which sought as well to facilitate local blacks in making their own media documenting the movement's activities and in using the licensing process to protest racist broadcasting by southern media outlets.[41] Nevertheless, I've chosen to concentrate on SCLC because that organization—particularly in its production of King as a media figure—clearly did the best job among major movement groups in using television to advance its aims, and because materials relating to SCLC's media strategy are more readily available than corresponding materials related to other groups. After a brief discussion of the Montgomery Bus Boycott, the context in which King and the movement discovered the importance of being mediated, I will consider two of the organization's most successful campaigns, those in Birmingham (1963) and Selma (1965), in order to illustrate how SCLC deployed the visuality of black performance in confrontations with segregationist power.

In Montgomery, King and the other leaders of the Montgomery Improvement Association (MIA) ran head-on into the problem of media representation almost immediately. David Garrow describes an early meeting of the boycott's organizers, in which

> Reverend Wilson reported that press photographers would be at the rally, and some ministers seemed reluctant to volunteer as speakers in light of that fact. E. D. Nixon angrily rebuked them. "Somebody in this thing has got to get faith. I am just ashamed of you. You said that God has called you to lead the people and now you are afraid and gone to pieces because the man tells you that the newspaper men will be here and your pictures might come out in the newspaper. Somebody has got to get hurt in this thing and if you preachers are not the leaders, then we have to pray that God will send us some more leaders."[42]

"Somebody has got to get hurt." Nixon's words indicate his assent to Reverend Wilson's premise that mediated visibility will indeed entail risk, possibly mortal risk. Indeed, the fact of being publicly identified as an organizer of the boycott might well have killed Nixon himself, as his home, along with King's, was bombed during the eleven-month protest. And being known by sight as well as by name would certainly increase the likelihood of harassment and attack. Nonetheless, something crucial in the history of the movement's relation to publicity happens in this moment: the terrifying leap of faith Nixon asks his colleagues to take here is precisely what allows King and his circle eventually to appreciate the uses to which having one's picture "come out in the newspaper" might be put.

Perhaps Nixon, an associate of A. Phillip Randolph and a longtime organizer, was thinking of Emmett Till, lynched the previous year in the Mississippi delta for allegedly addressing a white woman without observing the strict southern rules governing interracial speech. Till's murder provided a significant precedent for the Montgomery movement in two ways. First, Mamie Till Mobley, Till's mother, brilliantly insisted on iconizing the abused body of her son, demanding an open casket past which mourners in Chicago streamed for four days, and allowing *Jet* to use an image of Till's battered face, bloated and misshapen from river water, on its cover.[43] It would not be going too far to say that Mobley thus invented the strategy that later became the SCLC's signature gesture: literally *illustrating* southern atrocity with graphic images of black physical suffering, and disseminating those images nationally.[44] In addition, although Till's murderers, Roy Bryant and J. W. Milam, were acquitted of the crime, Till's trial provided the occasion for a coalescence of reporters covering a new beat: civil rights.[45] These reporters, many of whom worked for northern papers, provided abundant critical commentary on southern racial mores during the trial, thus signaling to astute black readers that they had a new ally in this national press corps.

Whether Nixon had Till in mind or not, he was proved correct in his assessment that, in addition to increasing black activists' vulnerability to racial terrorism, media attention could serve to protect them from it, as well as providing strategic information to local blacks. And despite the specter of "pictures in the newspapers" that loomed over the early MIA meeting, print media were not the only important sources of information in Montgomery, as the following anecdote, from Garrow, suggests:

Just as Nixon had hoped, Sunday morning's *Advertiser* featured an Azbell story headlined NEGRO GROUPS READY BOYCOTT OF CITY LINES. . . . The prominent news story had two immediate effects. First, Montgomery's white community was informed of the blacks' challenge. City Police Commissioner Clyde Sellers, a rabid racist, went on local television to denounce the effort and to say that Montgomery policemen would stand ready on Monday to assist those black citizens who wanted to ride the buses. . . . Second, the *Advertiser* story, plus Sellers' television pronouncement, reached many of Montgomery's black citizens, including some who had missed both the door-to-door leaflets and the Sunday morning announcements in most black churches. Nixon, who returned Sunday morning from his train run, and the other organizers were overjoyed at the unwitting assistance the whites had given them.[46]

Both television and the movement were new enough that Montgomery whites apparently didn't think to censor televised representations of the protest. Thus, throughout the boycott, local television played a crucial and unusual role by breaking the local newspapers' monopoly on information.[47] Both papers were owned by the same company; the less racist, the *Advertiser*, covered the movement only reluctantly and disparagingly. But, according to David Halberstam, news director Frank McGee, at Montgomery's NBC affiliate WSFA-TV, sympathized with the protesters' demands. Perhaps more to the point, he understood that he had a very good story on his hands, and covered it assiduously. Once the boycott became a national story, NBC agreed, often including McGee's reports from Montgomery on the network news.[48] Bridging local and national audiences, then, McGee's coverage allowed protesters to see themselves represented as social agents, both within Montgomery and within much larger struggles for human rights in the U.S. and internationally.[49] The capacity to *see* themselves—both figuratively and literally—as political actors was something long denied black activists in the South, where local papers generally refused to cover black protest.[50] Television coverage of the boycott thus helped bolster the boycotters' growing audacity in the face of racist retaliation and break the immobilizing fear of terrorist violence that had for decades prevented mass protest among southern blacks. As that fear dissipated, Fairclough notes, "the ministers began to enjoy their new role. By early 1956, the protest was attracting national and international publicity. . . . [I]nitially cagey about revealing their identities, they now enjoyed the prestige conferred by media coverage."[51]

None enjoyed that prestige more than King. He got the most of it, and there is wide consensus among both participants in and chroniclers of the movement that he was extremely savvy in its deployment.[52] Montgomery made him a national media star of sufficient magnitude that he continued to garner coverage even as SCLC struggled to find an agenda, a method, and an administrative structure during the late '50s. During this period, King continued to polish his on-air skills and to think about television's potential uses for the movement, imagining a weekly television show and a Billy-Graham-style "Crusade for Citizenship" that would "arouse the conscience of the nation through radio, TV, newspapers and public appearances of southern leaders as to conditions that exist, progress being made, and the responsibility of the entire nation to help ensure for Negro citizens these elementary rights."[53] In fact, the Crusade for Citizenship went forward, under the direction of Ella

Baker, but had only marginal effects. It was not until the apex of the Birmingham movement, in 1963, that the various ingredients enabling the movement's effective use of television would be collected.[54] Montgomery had yielded a number of these: the further consolidation of the civil rights press corps first assembled to cover the Till case; a telegenic leader; and a strategic understanding of the uses to which nonviolent protest and the self-iconization of black suffering might be put. The rest had yet to be assembled.

The first of these was well-organized press outreach, which was coordinated in Birmingham by Wyatt Walker, then SCLC's executive director. Walker held daily briefings for the press and helped journalists meet their deadlines by organizing the demonstration schedule around the time-consuming process of getting film from Birmingham to New York in time to air that night.[55] He also had a flair for the dramatic and clearly understood his task as producing spectacular racist violence against nonviolent black demonstrators. Thus he was not above expressing regret over Bull Connor's restraint early in the campaign, trying to provoke the Public Safety Commissioner's retaliation, and expressing delight at Connor's eventual decision to employ fire hoses and police dogs against marchers. As Fairclough notes, "the dogs and hoses were SCLC's best propaganda. Walker recalled how he told [James] Bevel 'to let the pep rally go on a while and let these firemen sit out there and bake in the sun until their tempers were like hair triggers.' According to James Forman of SNCC, when Walker watched the ensuing scenes replayed that evening on television, he jumped up and down in elation."[56]

Another of the ingredients in SCLC's successful deployment of television in Birmingham was a staff member with production experience in TV, and a thorough understanding of the medium's constraints and requirements. Before moving to Atlanta to work with SCLC, during his tenure at the National Council of Churches, Andrew Young had become interested in the power of visual media like film and television to influence by "control[ling] the image that appeared in the viewer's mind." Spurred by this interest, he became involved in the making of a weekly series produced jointly by the NCC and CBS called *Look Up and Live*. Young worked both behind and in front of the camera, learning that "television was demanding and unforgiving." He recalls, "We had sixty seconds to open and close the program. In that time, we had to get across the main point. . . . It couldn't be sixty-two seconds and it shouldn't be fifty-eight seconds."[57]

Young's training in formulating a visual message economically and efficiently contributed crucially to SCLC's campaign in Birmingham and its subsequent efforts. In particular, he refined the organization's publicity efforts and focused them more clearly on the needs of television news crews by inventing what later came to be known as the "sound-bite." In his words,

> At the Dorchester [planning] meeting [for the Birmingham campaign], I had impressed upon Martin the importance of crafting a message that could be conveyed in just sixty seconds for the television cameras. Martin picked it up right away, reciting to me a favorite saying of Dr. Benjamin Mays, President of Morehouse College:
>
>> One tiny little minute
>> Just sixty seconds in it
>> I can't refuse it
>> I dare not abuse it
>> It's up to me to use it
>
> . . . [W]hen I emphasized the need to have a message that we could convey in a matter of seconds, Martin would smile and say "One tiny little minute, just sixty seconds in it."[58]

There is little question that King was a receptive student of Young's media-relations pedagogy, or that the student could teach a few lessons of his own. King was keenly aware of the importance of the press to SCLC's success in Birmingham, going to jail on Good Friday to spark national interest in the campaign and agonizing over the movement's inability to generate coverage prior to movement stalwart James Bevel's innovation of the children's crusade.[59] King's phone conversation with Coretta Scott King from the Birmingham jail provides an excellent index of his preoccupation with keeping the movement in the news. As scholars of King note unfailingly, his primary interest was in ensuring that his wife told Walker that President Kennedy had called her to express concern over King's welfare in jail, so that Walker could tell reporters.[60]

The final ingredients contributing to the movement's successful use of television in Birmingham were supplied by James Bevel. As a college student in Nashville, Bevel had, with Bernard Lafayette, John Lewis, Diane Nash, and others, participated in the nonviolent sit-ins that desegregated the city's restaurants. In that capacity, he was one of the "stars" of the NBC *White Paper*, "Sit In." I will discuss this documentary more fully in Chapter 2; for now it suffices to say that Bevel's experience with "Sit In" produced certain insurgent knowledges about television that were extremely useful in Birmingham. First, as one of the earliest performers in the emerging genre of civil rights TV, Bevel understood well the mechanisms of political dramaturgy involved in "staging" a protest. And this understanding no doubt contributed to Bevel's audacious and risky conception of the children's marches. Faced with a shortage of adults willing or able to go to jail, Bevel was first among his cohort to imagine the practical and spectacular uses to which a mass performance of infantile citizenship might be put, in crowding Birmingham's jails and America's field of vision at the same time.[61] In addition, Bevel was able to imagine a television spectatorship comprised of to-be-mobilized blacks who would be recruited to the movement and prepared for nonviolent protest by televisual representation. He used "Sit In" as a training film in Birmingham (and elsewhere), thus routing black performance to potential black political agents through the medium of network television.

Clearly, the various innovations of Birmingham with respect to media relations reinforced each other in effecting a major shift in the culture of SCLC. During and after Birmingham, Walker, Young, Bevel, and King collaborated in elaborating innovative publicity techniques that placed the press, and particularly television, at the center of the organization's planning and strategies. SCLC operatives, though, knew enough to downplay the media's role in the movement. Noting that such an admission "likely would have made the movement, and Dr. King, appear considerably more 'calculating' than they wanted to seem," Garrow emphasizes that King's writing and speeches contain virtually no mention of media, save for allegorical references to visibility or light, "as when King spoke of 'the light of day' or the 'spotlight' that illuminated the evils of racist brutality."[62]

Despite its strategic silence about its publicity efforts, though, SCLC's 1965 Selma campaign dispels any doubts as to the media-centeredness of the organization's efforts.[63] The organization chose Selma not only because of the well-known intransigence of the Dallas County registrars with respect to registering black voters, but also because of the famously short fuse of Dallas County Sheriff Jim Clark and the proximity of Selma to network affiliates in Montgomery.[64] SCLC planners hoped that the combination would prove fortuitous. In Andrew Young's words, "The movement did not 'cause' problems in Selma. . . . [I]t just brought them to the surface where they could be dealt with. Sheriff Clark had been beating black heads in the back of the jail for years, and we're only saying to him that if he still wants to beat heads he'll have to do it on Main Street, at noon, in front of CBS, NBC, and ABC television cameras."[65]

In fact, the SCLC was sufficiently focused on its goal of providing the networks with Clark's racist performances that the staff decided, after the sheriff behaved mildly at the first demonstration, that they would move on to another town if he didn't react as expected the following day.[66] They needn't have worried. Clark returned to form the next day in a contretemps with veteran local activist Amelia Boynton in front of television cameras. In John Lewis's recollection, "Mrs. Boynton apparently moved too slowly for his tastes, and the next thing you knew he was manhandling her, really shoving and roughing her up. . . . You could hear the news photographers' cameras clicking, and I knew that now it was starting, that cycle of violence and publicity and more violence and more publicity that would eventually, we hoped, push things to the point where something—ideally, the law—would have to be changed."[67] Lewis's account suggests how thoroughly, by the time of the Selma campaign, his understanding of the movement's progress had become imbricated with his awareness of the coverage it garnered: what the memoirist recalls, many years later, is not finally the violence of this moment, but the moment's initiation of "that cycle of violence and publicity" that might force change.

Movement workers were elated: at the mass meeting that night, Ralph Abernathy, before a cheering crowd, proclaimed the sheriff an "honorary" civil rights worker for his service to the cause.[68] Abernathy's quip underscores the attention being paid to the coverage by the highest levels of the SCLC, attention further demonstrated by King's notes to Andrew Young from jail after his arrest on February 1, which read as though written by an accomplished public relations operative. The instructions King gave Young on February 2, titled "Do following to keep national attention focused on Selma," read, in part, "Keep some activity alive every day this week." Other points included "Follow through on suggestion of having a congressional delegation to come in for personal investigation. They should also make an appearance at mass meeting if they come"; "Seek to get big name celebrities to come in for moral support"; "Consider a night march to the jail protesting my arrest (an arrest which must be considered unjust). Have another night march to court house to let Clark show true colors."[69] In other words, King provides Young with specific examples of movement-generated content for the press—the congressional visit to Selma, the "big name celebrities," the night marches, and "Clark show[ing his] true colors"—even as he proposes a frame for the story with the parenthetical "an arrest that must be considered unjust."

On February 3, King laid out the next day's schedule for Young: "If all goes well get us out at 1:00 P.M. tomorrow. We will go directly to Federal Building to see Congressmen. Set press conference for 2:30. Prepare the kind of statement that I should read to press on release from jail. When it is definite that we are coming out let the press know the time so they will be on hand at the jail for our release." The stops on King's itinerary—coming out of jail, meeting the congressional delegation, and the press conference—would provide photo opportunities and thus satisfy King's demand for political showmanship: at the close of the note, King urges Young, "Also please don't be too soft. We have the offensive. It was a mistake not to march today. In a crisis we must have a sense of drama."[70]

King's concern with "drama" was a value that, by Selma, had clearly saturated the SCLC's political culture, a fact that is evidenced by C. T. Vivian's February 16 encounter with Jim Clark while leading a demonstration at the Dallas County courthouse. It was raining that day, and Vivian asked that those waiting to sign the Registrar's "appearance book" be allow to stand inside, out of the rain. When Clark refused, Vivian continued to bait him, comparing him to Hitler and his deputies to Nazis, all the while urging the television cameras across the street to capture the escalating confrontation.[71] The reporters became players in the scene when a cameraman switched on a light and Clark's anger was momentarily directed toward him; Selma historian Charles Fager reports that Clark yelled "Turn out that light or I'll shoot it out!"[72] When Clark could stand no more of Vivian's heckling, and with deputies trying to restrain him, he hit Vivian in the face in full view of the cameras and then went after the cameramen and reporters with a billy club.[73] When Vivian regained his feet, cameras recorded him exclaiming triumphantly, blood dripping from his mouth, "We're willing to be beaten for democracy, and yet you misuse democracy in these streets!" As Fager observes dryly, "This encounter made vivid television"[74] (fig. 1.1).

If Clark deserves coproducer credit with Vivian for their courthouse showdown, his own sense of drama may have overtaken the movement's during the encounter with marchers on the Edmund Pettus Bridge on "Bloody Sunday," March 7. I have found no evidence that movement strategists anticipated the intensity of the violence that Alabama state troopers and Clark's "posse" — the deputized racists who did much of the sheriff's dirty work — would visit on the protesters. Trapped by the line of troopers in front of them, with the Alabama River to their left and right, blacks were chased by mounted possemen, beaten bloody and broken by billy clubs, trampled by fleeing comrades, and blinded by tear gas. But Clark (and George Wallace, who dispatched the troopers) had intended this to be a live performance only: officials on the scene had pushed the cameras back far enough from the action that they, apparently unfamiliar with telephoto lenses, thought that the newsmen couldn't get "good" pictures. I will have more to say on the question of "good" pictures in a moment; I will merely note here that the pictures were good enough, at least, for ABC to interrupt its premiere broadcast of *Judgement at Nuremberg* with footage from Selma, confusing many viewers about the difference between the American South and Nazi Germany and setting a number of them on the road to Alabama.[75] They were good enough that SCLC lawyers entered the CBS footage into evidence at the hearings held by federal district court Judge Frank John-

FIGURE 1.1.
(top) Sheriff Jim
Clark threatens a
network reporter
with a billy club;
(bottom) Reverend
C. T. Vivian, just
after being hit by
Clark.

son to adjudicate the legality of the Selma to Montgomery march and
that the screening immediately preceded Johnson's ruling in favor of the
SCLC.[76] They were good enough for then-Selma Mayor Joseph Smither-
man to muse in retrospect, "I did not understand how big it was until I
saw it on television."[77] And they were good enough, according to the
CBS correspondent covering Selma, Nelson Benton, that "the word started
going around, around the [Alabama] statehouse, middle of the week,
and the phrase was 'There was too much film.' You know, that was the
phrase that the governor's people [were] using. 'Just too much film. Too
much film.'"[78]

"THE VEHEMENCE OF A DREAM"

I have argued that, for reasons of its own, network television made
common cause with the civil rights movement in its quest for a national
audience. I have argued as well that civil rights strategists, particularly

those associated with King's SCLC, proved remarkably adept both at providing visually dramatic and narratively coherent stories designed with the networks in mind, and at streamlining the logistics of the networks' incorporation of those stories into their narrative flows. In the process, I have attempted to disrupt the origin story that claims that African American representation on television derives solely from the stock types of minstrelsy and to begin to explain another kind of televisual traffic in black performance, one that usually fancies itself antiracist and tends to be marked by the generic admixture of information and entertainment forms.

I have tried to suggest as well some of the counterhegemonic uses to which the burden of liveness might be put by black subjects. For despite the falsity of liveness's promise of unmediated access to an extra-televisual real, liveness by its nature opens a space through which the occasional kernel of history sometimes propels itself, landing in the lap of the unsuspecting home viewer, if not unmediated then at least incompletely processed by television's narrative-making apparatus. Viewers are then left, briefly, to make their own narratives; on Bloody Sunday, the stories some of them told forced them out of their houses, onto buses or planes, or into cars, and on to Selma.

There is a good deal of discussion about the quality of the film shot by television cameras on the Edmund Pettus Bridge. Andrew Young notes, "After the beating on the bridge everyone knew about Selma, and for a very good reason: the brutality was fully captured by television news cameras on the other side of the bridge. The newsmen were situated behind the mass of troopers, and while the troopers had moved them back to where they thought they could not get good pictures, the scenes they captured were vivid."[79] Nelson Benton recalls, "I was pressing for more [air]time . . . because, under the criteria that we use, it was a hell of a good piece of film."[80] While Young is certainly correct that the footage was "vivid," Benton's claim is more puzzling because it is so obviously false. The film from Selma was not good film by the usual standards of television news, which tend to favor clarity and legibility: the respectful long shot of the President getting off a plane; the close-up of the neighbor amazed that the man living next door turns out to be a serial killer; or the witness at the scene of the accident describing the squeak of tires and the half-seen license plate. George B. Leonard came closer to the truth. As he described it at the time for the *Nation*, "The pictures were not particularly good. With the cameras rather far removed from the action and the skies partly overcast everything that happened took on the quality of an old newsreel. Yet this very quality, vague and half silhouetted, gave the scene the vehemence and immediacy of a dream."[81]

FIGURE 1.2.
Crisis coverage in
Selma.

Like the Rodney King video, which I discuss at greater length in chapter 3, the Selma footage is *not* good footage by the standards of television news, but it is exemplary footage by the standards of the privileged form of liveness that Mary Ann Doane had called crisis coverage.[82] Crisis coverage, like that from Selma, is marked narratively by ongoing conflicts, often political ones; it is marked visually by long static shots of nothing much happening, replaced suddenly by frenzied, oddly-framed or blurry images once the crisis begins to unfold (fig. 1.2). These visual markers, which often add up to one or another kind of illegibility, are in fact the formal markers of the political process that is unraveling before our eyes: the loss of the camera's control of the image is one of the things that tells the audience that political control, too, is up for grabs. In the process, the television narrator's drive to tell the story of the pictures is confounded and we find ourselves momentarily able to tell our own, and, in some cases, to dream a vehement dream.

Civil rights on TV
=new representation
of AFAMs in the media

CHAPTER TWO

The Double Life of "Sit-In"

IN THE PREVIOUS CHAPTER, I argued that network news organizations and major organizations of the civil rights movement shared an interest in ensuring that civil rights activities were televised and widely viewed. I also sketched in broad strokes both the industrial context in which news workers found themselves in the late 1950s, and the movement context in which media strategies were elaborated and revised. In this chapter, I undertake a similar inquiry with a narrower focus, scrutinizing a single text, the 1960 NBC *White Paper*, "Sit-In." After discussing in general terms the networks' turn toward documentary production in the late '50s and early '60s, and elaborating how "Sit-In" might have met some of NBC's industrial and economic needs at the moment it was produced, I will suggest through textual analysis that the documentary was also carefully—albeit rather counterintuitively—structured to meet some of the ideological needs of its producers and of the networks in general with respect to the then-emergent racial formations of the period.[1] In the second half of the chapter, I will consider the fact that "Sit-In" was taken up by movement activists as a training film, used to teach new recruits the techniques of nonviolent resistance. I will examine the record of the uses and meanings of this text for activist African Americans, inquiring what it was about "Sit-In" that allowed such an appropriation.

"SIT-IN"'S INDUSTRIAL CONTEXT

In the late 1950s and early 1960s, the networks found themselves in the midst of an intractable public relations crisis.[2] Public faith in the networks had been badly shaken by the quiz show scandals. In addition, as the networks standardized production methods and completed the transition from live production to filmed series, critics lamented the lack of program diversity. Critics accused the networks as well of allowing their profit motives to overtake their responsibilities in the public interest.

At the same time, the networks were also facing a new and potentially threatening regulatory climate at the Federal Communications Commission. As I discussed in the previous chapter, inquiries during this period into whether the network practice of option time constituted a violation of antitrust laws threatened an important source of network profits. In addition, hearings on the networks' programming practices underscored Congressional concern about the fate of public service programs.[3] And Kennedy's appointment of Newton Minow as FCC chair in 1961 put networks and affiliates on notice that the FCC was going to take an active interest in program content. Minow began his term with the famous speech to the 1962 National Association of Broadcasters, in which he likened television to a "vast wasteland."[4] The speech unabashedly valorized informational programming over the network's then-current penchant for westerns and crimes shows.

In this newly hostile milieu, the networks cast about for a solution to their regulatory and public relations woes. All came up with the same answer: prime-time documentaries. Through what Michael Curtin has called "flagship" documentary series—CBS Reports, NBC White Paper, and Bell and Howell Close-Up at ABC—the networks hoped to rebuild their credibility as truth-tellers and increase program diversity and public service programming at a stroke, thus answering critics both inside and outside of the government. In the process, they also hoped to make their news divisions more profitable by spreading the cost of global newsgathering over a greater number of program hours and demanding that news divisions earn their keep.[5]

"Sit-In," which aired December 20, 1960, was the second installment of the NBC White Paper series, and the fact that it was produced to serve NBC's public relations needs is clear. It treats a self-evidently serious and important topic of widespread and urgent public interest, thus balancing the network's entertainment offerings and ensuring program diversity. And it seeks to reestablish its network's credibility as a purveyor of truth chiefly through its deployment of NBC Nightly News coanchor Chet Huntley. Huntley, who introduces and concludes the program, epitomizes seriousness and deliberation as he places the Nashville sit-in movement within a "big picture." Immediately after the credits, we find him, seated in front of a control panel, shot in medium close-up.[6]

In 1954, the historic Supreme Court decision on public school desegregation presented that area of the United States traditionally called the South with its first region-wide crisis in race relations of the twentieth century. Six years later, in 1960, the South is again faced with a crisis in race relations of perhaps even greater significance: the sit-in movement. It comes at a time of sweeping social and political changes among the colored peoples of the world. And in our own country, it has challenged certain fundamental concepts of law, affected the conduct of national politics and is shaking the regional traditions of the South in an entirely new way. In this NBC White Paper, we shall examine the phenomenon of the sit-in, focusing on the one city where it had its clearest and most significant expression: Nashville, Tennessee.

Huntley, by virtue of his symbolic and literal placement at the "controls," is positioned to adjudicate the relative seriousness of "crises" in southern race relations, despite, or rather *because*, as the contortions of his phrasing establish definitively, he is not himself located in "that area of the United States traditionally called the South." Addressing a national audience, located only in the putatively neutral non-location of the television studio, he is granted a capacity for global and historical overview that allows him to link the sit-ins to "a time of sweeping social and political changes among the colored people of the world." From this properly national space, he is able to assess the effects of the sit-ins "in our own country," and pronounce that they were "most significant" in Nashville. In the control room, then, he floats above commerce and commercialism, above region and sectionalism, above politics.

Huntley's symbolic position is made even more clear by the next five shots, which appear under his voice-over: "In Nashville, on April 19th 1960, four thousand Negroes marched angrily on City Hall to bring to a climax two months of tension and violence that had enveloped the once-peaceful city. This is the story of those two months." The corresponding shots of the march, linked to the anchor by their correspondence to his voice-over, are all extreme long shots, shot from an extremely high angle, probably a building's rooftop. They render the marchers ant-like and swarming, while granting Huntley an empyrean view that gives new meaning to the notion of "voice of god" narration. This Huntley's-eye-view is then linked explicitly to Nashville's white power structure by a dissolve from the last shot of the marchers to a high-angle shot of the cityscape, which pans to a close-up of then-Mayor Ben West, who declares "I'm Ben West, and this is my city."

The opening of "Sit-In" is thus carefully calibrated to situate Huntley, and NBC, for which he is clearly intended to serve as a sign, as a kind of rational, disinterested, and "objective" authority, situated only by its evident proximity to the loci of power — over television, over Nashville. The opening is carefully calibrated, in other words, to restore critical and regulatory trust in NBC by exemplifying the organization's new commitment to a rigorous course of national pedagogy. But, for reasons discussed at length in the previous chapter, NBC's desire to portray itself as impartial must inevitably collide with the fact that the network, like its fellows, is anything but disinterested with respect to civil rights activism and its outcomes. To summarize briefly my argument in the previous chapter, all the networks had an interest in the abolition of marked sectional differences in the understanding of race and its meanings, because such differences impeded their ability to construct their address — and the address of their advertisements — as *national*. The networks thus participated quite actively, through texts like "Sit-In," in the movement's project of producing a new national consensus on race. The problem for "Sit-In," then, is how simultaneously to appear to be a paradigm of objective and trustworthy authority while at the same time supporting black activism against segregation in Nashville and elsewhere. The program accomplishes this delicate operation through a narrative logic of retrospection. "Sit-In" purports to show not what is happening, but what has already happened. In the process, it makes the Nashville movement's victories seem all but inevitable.

"Sit-In" Flashes Back

I have already mentioned that Huntley's introduction to "Sit-In" ends with the words "In Nashville, on April 19th 1960, four thousand Negroes marched angrily on City Hall to bring to a climax two months of tension and violence that had enveloped the once-peaceful city. This is the story of those two months." Huntley's words are followed immediately by a dissolve, the conventional filmic indicator of temporal ellipsis or shift. Indeed, this sequence comprises what Maureen Turim has called a "classic" flashback:

> In its classic form, the flashback is introduced when the image in the present dissolves to an image in the past, understood either as a story-being-told or a subjective memory. Dialogue, voice-over or intertitles that mark anteriority through language often reinforce the visual clues representing a return to the past.[7]

Indeed, the flashback that structures "Sit-In" as a whole, inaugurated by the words, "This is the story of those two months," is repeated, throughout the film, by other flashbacks-within-a-flashback. Several times, for example, interviewee Angeline Butler, an activist and Fiske student, introduces flashbacks of her own, appearing as a talking head that dissolves first to a workshop on techniques of nonviolent protest, then to the first sit-in, and finally to "our first really violent day," the day on which white protester Paul LaPrad was torn from his counter stool and beaten and kicked by segregationists.[8] In addition, the documentary is punctuated by persons affected by the campaign recalling their experiences: a white member of the biracial citizens' committee recalls its first meeting; the judge who heard the students' cases recalls being pressured from all sides; a downtown merchant recalls a month without many customers. Though the latter are not "classic" flashbacks, in Turim's term, they underscore just how thoroughly "Sit-In" is obsessed with retrospection.

What are we to make of these gestures? After all, the deployment of flashback is a high-risk proposition within a genre claiming a privileged relation to truth. For flashback is a cinematic device that has generally signified *either* history ("the shared and recorded past") *or* subjective memory (what Turim calls "the personal past").⁹ The structuring presence of flashback in "Sit-In" thus necessarily invites its viewers—who are presumably well-acquainted with the device's meanings—to interrogate the documentary's truth claims.

One reason why the film may be willing to take this risk is suggested by Curtin, who argues that, in their competition with entertainment programming for audiences, "documentary representations of important social issues were significantly influenced by the storytelling conventions of popular television," conventions themselves borrowed from Hollywood film. These included "considerations of plot, character, [and] pursuit of an affective response from audiences."¹⁰ Citing evidence of the dominance of commercial logic in documentary production at all three networks, Curtin builds a convincing case for the indebtedness of television documentary to the visual and narrative conventions of fictional television and classical Hollywood film: clearly drawn, intimate characterization; narrative structured by conflict among "characters" rather than social forces; continuity editing that obscures the text's manipulation of location and temporality; and high production values. It may be the case, then, that "Sit-In" was willing to structure its narrative in ways that resembled Hollywood fiction in order to insure its viability in a high-stakes ratings grab.

Clearly, though, there are other reasons as well. If the Nashville movement is "over," relegated definitively to the historical past, "Sit-In" can lend its successes an air of "inevitablity." In Turim's words,

> Another [of the ideological effects of the flashback] is to establish a certain view of historical causality and linkage. By presenting the result before the cause a certain logic of inevitability is implied; certain types of events are shown to have certain types of results without ever allowing for other outcomes other than the one given in advance.¹¹

This "logic of inevitability" has effects that, I argue, correspond neatly to NBC's desires as I've elaborated them. First, the structure of the flashback both complements and follows from the film's construction of Huntley's omniscience. He knows the entire story—its beginning, middle, and end—while we, presumably, don't. He is thus empowered to pick and choose among narrative strategies, conveying events in the order he chooses, and further undergirding the authority of his address in the process.

In addition, the "logic of inevitability" allows "Sit-In" to maintain its pretense toward objectivity while at the same time suggesting that the tactics used in Nashville—nonviolent direct action and economic boycott—are somehow "naturally" effective, and thus have a very good chance of working not only in Nashville, but throughout the South. As Huntley puts it,

> The confrontation at City Hall marked the turning point in Nashville. Soon afterward, a committee of merchant and student representatives met and worked out a plan for desegregating the six lunch counters that had been targets of the sit-ins. The economic boycott was withdrawn and Nashville became the first major city in the South to permit whites and Negroes to eat together in public places. The Nashville settlement was studied closely by other communities. By mid-summer a total of 27 cities had opened their lunch counters to all customers. There have been no disorders as a result, and none of the merchants affected has reported any loss in business.

Huntley here situates desegregation as the imminent *telos* of the forms of African American activism most palatable to powerful northern whites. The film is thus able quietly to lend its support to the integration of public accommodations through nonviolent means.

Finally, "Sit-In" needs the "logic of inevitability" implied by the flashback to sanction its ill-concealed contempt for the segregationist position, which receives remarkably little airtime. It needs that logic as well to entitle a camera rhetoric that subjects particular segregationists to obviously unsympathetic scrutiny. "Sit-In" shoots most such interview subjects in unforgivingly tight close-ups, their faces filling the frame, luridly, suggesting a lack of perspective, an over-proximity both to the camera and to their own self-serving desires.[12] Finally, the logic of inevitability allows the documentary further to impugn segregationists by depicting them in jail (a young white man who has beaten both a young white man who is a protester and a young black man who isn't), obviously lying (the local judge), employing questionable analogies ("a lion might like another lion more than he likes a bear"), or even offering their services as an "advisor to the black race" (a white man who notes that "the people of the South have always fed people who came to the back door asking for something to eat, but they have always reserved the right to eat only with invited guests"). Since history has proven them wrong, "Sit-In" seems to say, segregationists can be presented without much compunction as inarticulate, illogical, mendacious, or self-aggrandizing.

"Sit-In" as a Movement Text

I have situated "Sit-In" within the larger context of early-sixties documentary production and suggested some of the ways in which the film might have answered certain pressing public relations needs for its network. It answered other needs for its audience, though, some of which probably would not have been predicted by those who made it. For key movement operative Andrew Young, for example, who was working for the National Council of Churches in New York when "Sit-In" aired, the documentary served as a "call" for him and his wife, Jean, to return to the South: "As my family watched, we could literally feel God calling us back to the South."[13] Young discusses the experience of watching the program at length in both of his memoirs, *A Way Out of No Way* and *An Easy Burden*. These accounts offer an unusually detailed glimpse into the program's reception among progressive blacks.[14] In *An Easy Burden*, he writes,

> That night, NBC aired an hour-long program called "The Nashville Sit-In Story." We were very excited about watching the program. It was rare enough that black people were featured on television, but the story of the Nashville student action against segregation was extraordinary.[15]

After discussing the historical context of the Nashville movement, Young observes,

> The NBC profile featured several students who would continue in the civil rights movement: John Lewis, Bernard Lafayette, Jim Bevel, Diane Nash, [Angeline] Butler, and Marion Barry. I cannot overstate how impressive and inspiring these young men and women were to us. Their actions were rooted in deep personal faith and conviction. While the Montgomery bus boycott was a noncooperation with segregation, and in a sense consisted of passive nonviolence, the sit-ins were a direct, nonviolent confrontation with segregation."[16]

Young continues, Diane Nash "spoke with great clarity in the television piece, and that clarity of purpose would become a trademark of her leadership." And he singles out a young Nashville minister, Kelly Miller Smith, who would become an important part of the civil rights struggle there. Smith, Young notes,

> opened the television program and set the moral context. He said that Nashville was called the Athens of the South. Like Athens, Nashville was a place of great glory and tragedy: glory was its university — Vanderbilt — and its "tragedy was its race relations." It was powerful, but not threatening; rather he spoke with tremendous compassion, even sadness and regret.[17]

Young concludes, "When the television program ended, Jean and I knew that it was time to return home, to the South. It really didn't require any discussion. . . . We were committed to living and working in the South, and we realized that the moment had come." Young left the National Council shortly thereafter to run citizenship training and leadership development schools in the South.

Obviously, Young's memories of "Sit-In" were written at considerable distance from the experience of watching the program, and are crafted to serve particular rhetorical purposes within his own texts. But they can still teach us something about the spectatorial practices the film engendered. First, and crucially, Young frames the documentary in a racialized televisual context in which it was unusual to encounter *any* blacks — particularly blacks protesting segregation — on television. He thus points to the kind of doubled impact civil rights programming may have had for black viewers at this historical juncture. In addition, Young remembers most clearly the "impressive and inspiring" students who appeared in "Sit-In," many of whom came to be Young's close collaborators in the movement. He makes no mention of the whites who appeared, and particularly elides Huntley in his characterization of Kelly Miller Smith as "open[ing] the television program and set[ting] the moral context." In thus emphasizing "the moral context," rather than the historical or global context Huntley seeks to elaborate, Young suggests that religious blacks may have understood the significance of the Nashville movement in rather different terms than those offered by the program itself. By writing Huntley (and other whites) out of "Sit-In," in other words, Young offers a resistant reading of the text that hints at the specific interpretive practices of at least some members of the African American community.

Young clearly believed that other blacks would react to "Sit-In" much the way he did, for he used it as part of the curriculum of the citizenship school he ran at the Dorchester Center in Georgia with Septima Clark, Dorothy Cotton, and Bernice Robinson in the early 1960s. The citizenship schools recruited community leaders throughout the South, brought them to the center, and taught them literacy skills, civics, and organizing techniques so that they could teach others what they had learned.[18] In Young's words, the program sought "to establish voter registration using a few key people in 188 crucial counties that had black majorities across the Deep South but almost no black registered voters. Our hope was that the first people registered would in turn begin registration campaigns in their own counties." Young describes the first day of each week-long training program:

> Our evening presentation was . . . "The Nashville Sit-In Story." The NBC program that drew me to the South also inspired countless others. The genius of that program was that it let the students tell their own story, and that story was a powerful inspiration to the participants in our citizenship schools. We wanted to give our students a sense that people had power and could change things without guns and without money.[19]

Just as Young was using "Sit-In" in the citizenship schools, by late 1961 SNCC workers in Mississippi were also using the film to recruit young people in Jackson to their direct action campaigns. This is confirmed by the 1961–62 correspondence exchanged between Fred Halsted of the Militant Labor Forum and the SNCC offices in Atlanta. Halsted writes:

I am writing you in reference to your film "The White Paper" which we are interested in showing at one of our forums. Would it be possible for you to loan us a copy of this during the latter part of January or the first part of February? If there are any charges for mailing, etc. we would be happy to pay for them.[20]

An unsigned carbon of the reply from SNCC states

Dear Mr. Halsted,
We do have a copy of the Nashville Sit-In story which we are using in the state of Mississippi. We are contacting our staff people there to see if it is possible to send it to you around the end of January. Since they have constant demand for it there, we certainly cannot promise any possible use at this time. You may expect to hear from us shortly. Please keep in touch.
Sincerely,
Charles McDew, Chairman
James Foreman, Executive Secretary[21]

The reply has been copied to Diane Nash in Jackson, where she was working with James Bevel and Bernard Lafayette to pry open one of the areas of the South most closed to blacks.[22] Movement historians and memoirists confirm that Bevel also used "Sit-In" in the Birmingham and Selma campaigns.[23] Given that I have thus far characterized "Sit-In" as a text designed to serve NBC's needs, what was it about the documentary that opened it to such persistent and thoroughgoing appropriation by civil rights activists?

"Sit-In" and Black Idiom

While the documentary's general sympathy toward the Nashville movement was certainly a factor in "Sit-In"'s apparently positive reception among activist or proto-activist blacks, several sequences may have had more to do with the documentary's appropriation by the movement than the text's overall tone. These sequences mobilize black idiom in ways that may have been scarcely legible to whites, and that may have allowed black audiences to feel singularly addressed by the program. "Sit-In," in other words, frequently breaks the rule cited by Curtin in his discussion of documentary address to black audiences. "As early as 1957," Curtin writes, a CBS study of documentary viewers recommended that the programs address themselves to a mass audience in order to connect with the largest number of viewers. "It is necessary to provide a broad basis for viewer involvement," argued the report, "Therefore, social and political problems pertaining to a minority should always be presented in terms of their importance to the majority."[24]

Such address, Curtin notes, placed the black viewer as "*eavesdropping* on a discussion of his or her economic and human rights."[25] Indeed, many civil rights documentaries are structured in precisely this way. But "Sit-In" sometimes addresses blacks directly, even at the risk of bypassing or bewildering white audiences in the process.

One such moment occurs at the very beginning of the program. The very first shot of "Sit-In" depicts two black men being led out of a lunch counter by police while a mostly white crowd looks on. The next fourteen shots comprise a montage under a nondiegetic voice-over. The shots depict, on one hand, black protesters being arrested, carrying signs ("Do Not Patronize F.W. Woolworth," "We simply want equal rights," "All are free or none are free," "Support Integration"), and passing out leaflets, and, on the other, white police doing the arresting, white spectators looking on, and white shoppers accepting or refusing the leaflets. The voice, which is never given a face by the film, speaks in a timbre and dialect clearly coded as that of a southern black man, intoning the following in cadences drawn from the revival meeting or the work song:

> My brothers, I'm glad, I'm glad to have the opportunity to tell people today that they're sleeping in a dangerous time. Rise, rise, rise, rise. I'm hearing me all of these things today. I feel so glad that I've got the opportunity to tell, tell the interested: run, run, run, run, run. Mens and womens that hasn't made a start to go before, to put up and do something for your race: wake up, wake up. Go and make a start and see if God will take a hold of you.

The montage is edited to the cadence of the voice-over of this absent speaker who addresses not the white opinion leaders *NBC White Paper* imagines as its audience, but precisely those potentially insurgent black subjects whom Young or Bevel hoped to involve in the movement.

The speaker is peripheral to the documentary in that this sequence appears before the credits, before the start of the film proper. He is marginalized in not being identified, or even made visible. But he also occupies a privileged position as the first voice we hear. And his voice broadens the class address of the film among blacks, not only in its regional and dialectical markedness, but also through its association with a striking formal feature of this sequence: the cut between the words "dangerous" and "time" in the phrase "sleeping in a dangerous time" juxtaposes a shot of women (two black, one white) with shopping bags crossing through the frame in opposite directions with a shot of two police officers holding open the door of a paddywagon for another woman. On one hand, this cut suggests the connection between consumer identity and social activism that the film will later make explicit in its discussion of the successful black boycott of downtown stores that Huntley describes as blacks' "ultimate weapon" against segregation. On the other hand, the editing suggests as well that shopping — and more broadly the consumer identity that the film celebrates as the crucial underpinning of black political aspirations — may itself constitute a treacherously bourgeois somnolence, particularly with respect to the working-class blacks whom the speaker implicitly represents. The ambiguity of this cut, and the markedness of the speaker's idiom surrounding it, open "Sit-In" to precisely the kinds of audiences Young sought to bring to the Dorchester Center: indigenous, resistant, "without guns and without money."

Another of the sequences mobilizing black idiom is the scene to which my students always object as a gratuitous example of African American performance embedded into the film's ostensibly political narrative: a young student in a Fiske gymnasium sings "Day-O" (or "The Banana Boat Song") to reenact the singing that kept the group's spirits high in jail. To some extent, indeed, my students are correct; this is a gratuitous moment. But it is something else, as well. I would guess that progressive black audiences would have read it also as an allusion to movement stalwart Harry Belafonte's performance of the same song in *Island in the Sun*, the 1957 miscegenation film that also starred Joan Fontaine, James Mason, and Dorothy Dandridge. Part of the cycle of what Thomas Cripps has called "Hollywood message movies," *Island in the Sun* featured two interracial romances and was widely banned throughout the South; the legislature of the state of South Carolina, in fact, considered passing a law that would have fined the owners of theaters showing the film $5000.[26] "Day-O"'s appearance in "Sit-In" thus reminds its viewers that "Sit-In" will almost certainly encounter the same hostile reception that *Island in the Sun* encountered in the South. More crucially, it resituates Belafonte's earlier film work as cultural work for the movement, while placing the student-singer with Belafonte in a larger tradition of counter-hegemonic African American performance.[27] Within the contexts of the Selma or Birmingham campaigns, the sequence functions pedagogically for young African Americans — who were, after all, the constituency Bevel used the film to recruit — teaching them about a tradition of such performance and inviting them to join that tradition as active participants. Through a system of specifically African American "star" identification, with Belafonte, the young singer, or Bevel himself, "Sit-In" thus produced new performers in the civil rights "drama."

Because "Sit-In" appears quite early in the cycle of network documentaries, it displays quite clearly the traits desired by the networks in such texts, particularly with respect to the ostentatious display of seriousness and journalistic "professionalism." But because "Sit-In" is a *civil rights* documentary, and because the outcome of civil rights activism was something with which NBC believed its own fate—economic and ideological—to be deeply bound, "Sit-In" is also a profoundly complex and overdetermined text, needing constantly to balance its commitment to objectivity with its desire to situate the Nashville movement as always-already successful. And perhaps because of this balancing act, and because "Sit-In" was made before the generic conventions of the civil rights documentary had been firmly established, "Sit-In" is a strikingly open text in its discursive strategies and address. It was this discursive and ideological openness that allowed "Sit-In"'s appropriation by movement operatives. In movement contexts, spectatorship of "Sit-In" yielded in turn new forms of black counterperformance.

CHAPTER THREE

King TV

RODNEY KING LIVE

IN THIS CHAPTER, I consider a set of racially charged televisual texts located at the nexuses of "fictional" and "nonfictional," of "live" and "recorded" and of the quotidian and the special. These texts are George Holliday's videotape of the beating of Rodney King; CNN's April 29, 1992 coverage of the Simi Valley verdict and its aftermath; and the 1992 season premieres of two established prime-time network series popular in the late 1980s and early 1990s — *L.A. Law* and *Doogie Howser, M.D.* Together, these texts — which we might call "King TV" — make up an archive that I will glean for evidence in considering two related hypotheses. First, the new racial hegemony of the 1980s — forged by the Reagan-Bush administration and network television, and described so richly by cultural critics Herman Gray in *Watching Race* and Jimmie L. Reeves and Richard Campbell in *Cracked Coverage* — continued to have lasting effects on cultural understandings of law, order, and race in the 1990s. Second, Reaganist understandings of race proceeded from a relentless *criminalization* of blackness, thus rendering law enforcement policy a crucial site for struggles over African American civil rights and signaling the importance of television's mediations of law and criminal justice for an understanding of the racial politics of the 1990s.

I read these texts by taking up more directly the question of liveness and African American representation I broached in chapter 1. I suggested there that we might understand liveness in a double sense. In the first sense, liveness describes both certain technical aspects of the televisual apparatus and the extrapolation of those aspects into an "ideology" of television emphasizing the putative immediacy, transparency, and presence of the medium's representations. In the second sense, liveness describes a specific racial imperative, one in which persons of color represented on television act as bearers of liveness on the medium's behalf. That the double meaning of liveness will yield contradictory effects is evident in the figure of Rodney King, who was given this burden of liveness even though he was nearly dead.

I will return to the possibility of reconciling these two senses of liveness shortly. For now, though, let me provide a very brief account of how the term "liveness" functions for one of its theorists, Jane Feuer.[1] In her influential 1983 article, Feuer notes that some commentators have suggested that television, by virtue of its capacity to record and transmit images simultaneously, is *ontologically* live, offering an immediacy and presence afforded by no other medium.[2] Feuer opposes the ontological reading by claiming rather that liveness is an organizing *ideology* of the medium, enabling it to claim that its discourse is equal to "the real."[3]

For Feuer, the importance of liveness as an ideology is marked by its omnipresence:

> as television in fact becomes less and less a "live" medium in the sense of an equivalence between time of event and time of transmission, the medium in its own practices seems to insist more and more upon an ideology of the live, the immediate, the direct, the spontaneous, the real. This is true of both program formats and metadiscourse (reference to the "Golden Age" of live television, "Live from New York, it's Saturday night," the many local spots glorifying "instant" camera news coverage, "live" coverage of the Olympics, etc.).[4]

Television's insistent invocation of its own liveness works ideologically to undergird the medium's real, hidden claim: "from an opposition between live and recorded broadcasts," Feuer goes on, "we expand to an equation of 'the live' with 'the real.' Live television is not recorded, live television is alive; television is living, real, not dead."[5]

One of hegemony's most delicate operations, it seems to me, is to render those whom society has most violently assaulted, both physically and culturally, alive again *within representation,* where intractable social problems such as race relations can be more easily solved.[6] And I would maintain more particularly that television's imperative to establish its own liveness by representing live and authentic African Americans on screen is one of the ways in which television fulfills this hegemonic function. To put it more bluntly, as one of the chief mechanisms in the reproduction of racial hegemony, television's depictions of "live" blacks tend to proliferate just as dead black bodies are piling up. Television's own liveness, which is constituted in significant measure through such "authentic" racialized depictions, may thus be bound quite tightly to the maintenance of America's still-violent racial hierarchies.

LIVENESS: AN IDEOLOGY OF TELEVISION AND RACE

As an ideology, then, both of television and of race, liveness was been crucial to the effectivity of King TV. Holliday's video — not live, of course, but taken at first to be the very epitome of liveness — certainly owes its existence to liveness's dual impulse: to represent "fully" a scandalous event that might otherwise be edited or censored, and to render live in representation a black body, King's, which might plausibly be dead by the end of the tape. And, indeed, the tape was widely received as live in precisely these ways, both by television audiences who saw parts of it at home on local and then national news, and by the prosecution as they prepared for the trial of King's assailants. Thus, in the Simi Valley trial, the liveness of the tape—its claims to presence, immediacy, and the "real"—persuaded prosecutors that it wouldn't be necessary to produce a reading of the video to counter that advanced by the defense. As Judith Butler has pointed out in "Endangered/Endangering: Schematic Racism and White Paranoia,"

> what the trial and its horrific conclusions teach us is that there is no simple recourse to the visible, to visual evidence, that it still and always calls to be read, that it is already a reading, and that in order to establish the injury on the basis of visible evidence, an aggressive reading of the evidence is necessary.[7]

The generalized misapprehension of the power of the visible that Butler correctly identifies here was, I suggest, further overdetermined in this case by the ideology of liveness: the prosecution's faith in the video's liveness, and its consequent overconfidence in the video's presumedly privileged relation to the real, persuaded them that they could rely on the self-evidence of visuality.

In national coverage of the rebellion itself, at a moment in which the codes of liveness crossed with those of crisis and catastrophe coverage, liveness served as well to signal the scale of the events, to alert the TV audience to their importance for the life of the nation. For although, as Feuer suggests, liveness permeates television's address and can be found everywhere on TV virtually at all times, liveness also serves, during crisis or catastrophe, as a marker of the exceptional event: in the commonplace televisual attention-getter, "We go live to the scene," the scene we go live to is a place where something unusual is happening. And when the medium, in another attention-getting ploy, remarks upon its own liveness, with a graphic that says "live" in the corner of the screen, it's specifying its discourse as different from the more usual fare of recorded programming interspersed by live announcements, or, in news programming, by the direct address of the anchorperson.[8] On U.S. television, events that justify this kind of interruption of the standard programming schedule are generally understood to be national crises. Indeed, this exceptional liveness has been, since the civil rights movement, that which both designates and constitutes such events in the U.S. For a few examples from the past decades, consider the Thomas/Hill hearings, the Waco standoff, the first World Trade Center bombing, the

"liveliness"
= makes us think its true

Oklahoma City bombing, the course of O. J.'s white Bronco, and, most recently, the events of September 11, 2001 and the subsequent "war on terrorism."

In addition to designating events in Los Angeles as worthy of national attention, the liveness of the rebellion coverage also served particular functions within the television industry at this moment, occurring as it did just as the boundaries of liveness, fictionality, and the real were being actively reorganized. In the early 1990s, television news organizations were considering the limitations and advantages of using amateur tapes. At the same time, network entertainment divisions searched for more ways to exploit the profit potential of "home video." In the wake of the Simi Valley verdict, TV news used its live coverage of the rebellion to reclaim for itself the functions of immediacy and presence that Holliday's video, and other amateur video like it, threatened to usurp. If the very rawness of Holliday's tape had established its "authenticity," and if Holliday's fortuitous presence at the scene served as a powerful if implicit indictment of TV news' claims to timely ubiquity, then TV news reactivated and reappropriated the prestige-function of liveness with its coverage of the verdict's aftermath. TV news effected this recovery in two ways: by insisting, at least in the hours immediately following the verdict, on its utter counterintuitiveness, and thus shoring up the ideology of liveness as common sense; and by narrating the production of its own images as an example par excellence of daredevil news-gathering, remarking ceaselessly on the potential dangers to their personnel "on the scene."

In reclaiming liveness for itself, TV news coverage of the rebellion reasserted its own authority in a particularly pernicious way. Since much of the live coverage of the rebellion was shot from helicopters, live television fulfilled its function of promoting national unity-in-diversity by aligning the view afforded by its cameras with the perspective of the police who regularly patrol South Central in similar helicopters.[9] This gaze policing Los Angeles in flames was only occasionally interrupted by a view originating on the ground. These choices were, of course, not merely "practical" but rhetorical and political as well. They determined what liveness made visible—primarily massive "property damage," which was, after all, President Bush's first concern[10]—and what liveness persistently refused to see—such as the racial and ethnic diversity of the "looters" and the fact that many of them were looting and distributing basic necessities like diapers and food.[11]

Liveness increasingly generates its own fictional recyclings, which work through and reimagine both the contemporary nation and its history. Many examples of this representational nexus might be adduced: the versions of previous decades offered by *China Beach*, *I'll Fly Away*,

That '70s Show, and soon, we're promised, *That '80s Show*; the "ripped from the headlines" aesthetic pioneered by the *Law and Order* franchise; representations of U.S. institutions in NBC's *The West Wing* and CBS's *First Monday*. Though many arguments have been made about the tendency of television to cannibalize its own images and stories, most critics have focused on strategies of "recombination" among fictional forms.[2] In the rest of this chapter I want to consider the recirculation of nonfictional liveness in King TV's fictional texts, interrogating the effects of this intertextual interface and arguing that we can discern in these conversations a struggle among televisual forms and genres to represent race and the nation. Fictional forms such as the sitcom and the prime-time drama produce their own relevance to national life by appropriating and recirculating liveness. In the process, they must inscribe its limits.

L.A. Law and Televisual Justice

The 1992 premiere of *L.A. Law*'s penultimate season cannibalizes liveness and its purported access to the "real" in hopes that the immediacy of liveness will provide some sense of urgency to its own plots, and thus spur flagging viewer interest in the series. This appropriation of "real life" is of course nothing new for the series: it pioneered the "ripped-from-the-headlines" aesthetic, which has become standard television fare in the years since *L.A. Law*'s 1986 premiere. And the series had taken up the question of Rodney King's beating in an episode from the 1991–92 season, in which Jonathan Rollins defends a black man who led police on a high-speed chase by claiming that his client's repeated exposure to the video on television had plausibly made him fear for his life at the hands of the LAPD.

The 1992 premiere stages its appropriation of liveness by worrying the questions posed by the verdict and its aftermath both explicitly and implicitly. I'll return in a moment to the ways in which this episode stages explicitly the interface of its characters with the concrete practices of the uprising, persistently placing white bodies as the victims par excellence of urban violence. First, though, I want to discuss a subplot that more obliquely takes up the intersections of race, representation, and the law. Arnie Becker, the sleazy divorce attorney who has wanted for several seasons now to move into the practice of entertainment law, is thrown a placating bone by his partners: he is representing an amusement park employee named Champion who has been fired from his job of dressing up as Homer Simpson because he became ill, took off the Homer-head of his costume, and vomited where park visitors could see him.[13] He has been fired, in other words, for "breaking the illusion" associated with his character, and he is suing "Familyland" in an attempt to get his job back.

The explicit function of this subplot is comic relief: we are treated to lots of Homer-style humor and asked to entertain the spectacle of this case, which is completely ridiculous. The plot also alludes nostalgically to many earlier *L.A. Law* plots from other seasons, and thus reminds audiences of the series' better days. But it also serves as a site in which a number of issues central to *California v. Powell* may be posed, transmuted, and resolved. The Familyland case against Champion hinges, for example, on a videotape, taken by a park visitor, of Champion collapsing and vomiting. Against Arnie's objections, Familyland's attorney introduces the tape and claims, in a parody of the prosecution in the Simi Valley case, that this evidence establishes unproblematically Champion's transgression. And Arnie's closing argument mimics the LAPD officers' defense perfectly:

> Ladies and gentlemen, this case is about perception. Let's also talk about reality. Fifteen seconds of tape is hardly representative of Mr. Champion's nineteen years at Familyland. What occurred before that camcorder was turned on, or after it was turned off? What are we missing here?

The substitution of Champion for King's assailants is crucial to the larger work of this episode, because of how this substitution situates embodiment and especially physical pain. *L.A. Law* perfectly extends the logic of the officers' defense, which hinged on the displacement of Rodney King's body, of Rodney King's pain, by the potential for the officers' pain: they had to beat him in order to prevent him from beating them.[14] Arnie's case neatly sidesteps even the necessity for such substitution by making Champion's "crime" self-evidently victimless, and self-evidently the result of his body's own pain. And simultaneous with its replacement of the black body in pain with the white one, the episode dramatically lowers the stakes. The only thing Arnie is defending, after all, is the right of incompetent white masculinity (i.e., Champion) to represent itself as larger-than-life incompetent white masculinity (i.e., Homer Simpson): more interesting, more entertaining perhaps, but still recognizable. Since Arnie is not, for example, defending the right of incompetent white masculinity to police and brutalize the bodies of people of color, the ideological move here is to reenact the logic of the Simi Valley trial in a context in which the outcome hardly matters—even, it seems, to the participants, for Champion himself disappears from the courtroom during Arnie's summation.

In the episode's more explicit engagements with the uprising, outcomes clearly matter: the question to be asked, of course, is to whom they matter, and how, and why. Here again, *L.A. Law* borrows the strategy of the officers' defense by fixating obsessively on the threat that people of color pose to white bodies. Three of the episode's subplots bear this out. In the first, assistant district attorney Zoë Clemmons comes home from the hospital to recover from a gunshot wound sustained in connection to a case in which her boss, a black woman, asked her to perjure herself. The scene I'm most interested in occurs after Zoë and Tommy Mullaney (Zoë's ex-husband and MacKenzie, Brachman associate) have a fight, and Zoë, still debilitated by her injury, leaves Tommy's apartment to brave the riot, claiming, "I know what it's like to get shot; I know what it's like to be dead." Later, she returns with Chinese take-out to find Tommy watching a "live" broadcast of a Tom Bradley news conference in which Bradley is discussing the deployment of the National Guard. Tommy turns off the television and Zoë explains why she's come back: "I was sitting in my apartment listening to the helicopters and the sirens and the gunshots, and the more I listened, the more afraid I got. And so I decided that the best way to combat my fears is just to live my normal life." At this point Zoë confesses to Tommy that she "deserved to get shot" as punishment for her perjury, and that she was "really disappointed" not to have had the classically mass-mediated near-death experiences — "seeing auras, leaving [one's] body" — because she felt "like I hadn't earned the privilege." With this, she turns to Tommy and asks, "Do you want to see my scar?" When he assents, she stands, opens her dress and takes the bandage off her chest. Tommy kisses the wound as a sultry saxophone — the feature of the *L.A. Law* soundtrack that serves as the series' most durable signifier of an imminent sexual encounter — becomes audible. Tommy and Zoë exchange a meaningful look. They kiss.

The civic drama of the rebellions is here reoriented in relation to Zoë's role in another municipal theatrical. Many of the elements — deceit, corruption, gunshots — are the same, and in both scenarios, the question to be adjudicated is how Zoë will live her "normal life." More to the point, the pathos of her guilt leaves no room for those for whom "helicopters, sirens, gun shots" constitute precisely the stuff of "normal life" under the regime of the same LAPD on whose behalf Zoë, as district attorney, must work. From the broadcast of the Bradley news conference, to the closing kiss, this scene moves ever inward: from civil unrest, to civic corruption, to the traumatized white body, to the healing powers of bourgeois white heterosexuality.

But if bourgeois white heterosexuality is situated in the Tommy/Zoë subplot as that which heals or redeems the traumatic encounter between the white body and urban unrest, the second subplot, involving Douglas, establishes bourgeois heterosexuality as urban unrest's first casualty.

In this plot, Douglas stops at a liquor store on the way to his wedding (in a link with the Tommy/Zoë subplot, Douglas is getting remarried to his ex-wife, Sheila) to buy some champagne. As he enters the store, we hear a TV in the background broadcasting local news of the looting: "What seems to have begun as loosely organized protests against that not-guilty verdict has in some cases. . . ." The voice of the oblivious Douglas at this point dominates the soundtrack, drowning out the television. He approaches the Asian shopkeeper, asking "Is this the best champagne you carry?" But the merchant has eyes only for the TV, which promises to "go now to our aerial reporter live from South Central." Seeing that the looting is spreading to his own neighborhood, he says, "Oh, trouble, big trouble," as Douglas tries to get his attention: "Say, could you put this in a box? . . . I'm running late. I'd appreciate you picking up the pace." At this point, the merchant disappears behind the counter, as Douglas calls to him, "And while you're back there, a bow would be nice." The merchant returns with a shotgun, and Douglas, misunderstanding the man's intention to protect him from the "trouble" that is, in the merchant's words, "too close for comfort," tries to appease him: "Forget the bow. I was way out of line." The shopkeeper's instruction — "Leave now. Hurry" — is punctuated by the sound of breaking glass, as a barely differentiated mass of black and Latino bodies surges past the impeccably tuxedoed Douglas (fig. 3.1).

Here the menace lurking at the margins of Zoë's attack is thoroughly literalized. It's tempting to read Douglas's presence here as punishment for the insufferable way he treats the owner of the store — as punishment, in other words, for his snobbishness and his entitlement, just as Zoë may have been shot as "punishment" for her perjury. But such a reading would be undermined by the further development of this subplot: later in the episode, after he has been picked up by the LAPD for, ironically enough, looting, Douglas is faced with the necessity of warding off the aggressive sexual advances of a black man while he's being held by police. Here *L.A. Law* refigures the scary mobility of Rodney King's sexuality, the scary mobility marked densely by King's purportedly inexplicable behavior upon getting out of his car after the chase: "shaking his behind" at the assembled officers.[5] For Douglas, faced with the much more legible version of King's behavior that *L.A. Law* imagines, class privilege serves as the last line of defense: after spitting on his assailant, who recoils, he yells, at him and any other potential attackers within earshot, "I'm supposed to be at the Bel Air Hotel, with my wife, having room service. I love room service. The next miscreant that so much as looks at me is a dead man." Douglas's outburst is ostensibly played for laughs, and its "humor" thus serves as an alibi for its astounding classism. In other words, this moment suggests self-iron-

FIGURE 3.1. Douglas encounters a mass of black and Latino bodies.

ically, but suggests nonetheless, that class privilege, rather than generating urban unrest, should be clung to as a bastion against "miscreants."

This question of punishment culminates in the final subplot I'll discuss. Stuart Markowitz is driving to Douglas's ill-fated wedding in his gold Lincoln Town Car. Impatient, honking at the other drivers, he turns off a crowded surface street onto a side road, and finds himself in a black and latino working-class neighborhood in which a menacing group of men of color obstructs his passage (fig. 3.2). They attack his car, break the windows, drag Stuart from the car, and beat him with bricks and baseball bats. Most of the shots of the beating—many of which work more or less self-consciously to reframe the images of Holliday's video in lurid color and better focus—are taken from two alternating angles: high-angle shots that allude to the helicopter's-eye-view of liveness in general and to the footage of the Reginald Denny beating in particular, and medium close-ups, mostly of blows connecting with Stuart's body, shot from ground level (fig. 3.3).

After witnessing the horrors of this scene, it's hard to remember Stuart's impatience, and the contrast between his enormous luxury car and the neighborhood he was driving through. And after listening to Ann Kelsey (Stuart's wife) ask Leland at the hospital, "Why would

FIGURE 3.2. Stuart menaced by men of color.

somebody do this to such a gentle soul?" our amnesia is further reinforced. In the closing scene of this subplot, we learn that Stuart is suffering from that classic TV trauma, "massive brain damage." When he
recovers consciousness, looks at Ann, and calls her "Mom," *L.A. Law*
delivers its crowning blow, deploying melodramatic codes to ensure
that, in this episode at least, the spectacle of Stuart's impairment within
the family will effectively displace our memory of his breathtakingly
entitled sense that he might superimpose himself anywhere on the city's
geography, at any time, without risk.

Each of these three subplots engages questions of agency, punishment,
and white guilt. And each of these plots situates those questions in relation to others about how the nature and status of white bourgeois heterosexuality—the default mode of adult sexuality in mass-mediated culture—might be altered or perverted via its contact with its racial,
sexual, and class others. In the bizarre sexual iconography of Zoë's encounter with Tommy, for example, the scar she reveals to him stands in
for the nipple that can't be shown within the codes of network "stan-

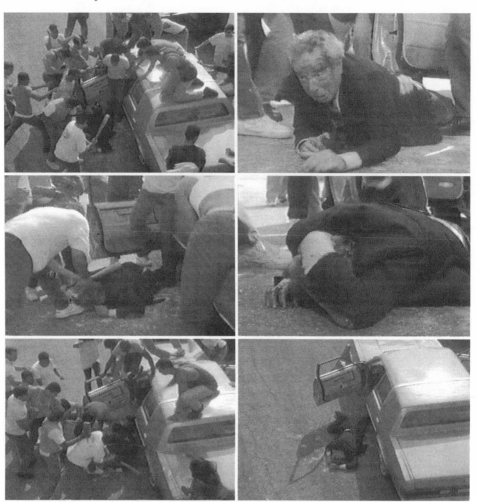

FIGURE 3.3. Stuart is dragged from his car and beaten.

dards," thus establishing a circuit in which the heterosexual rendezvous, inaugurated and enabled by Zoë's to-be-looked-at-ness, seems to require that the body that is revealed must also be damaged. In addition, Douglas's scene of public heterosexualization—his marriage—is deferred by his encounter with the urban sublime. In case we missed this point, the episode provides an explicit scene in which the specter of interracial homosexual rape follows directly from this deferral. Finally, Stuart's reduction, by urban violence, from loving husband to helpless child aligns bourgeois marriage with incest. White bodies and white middle-class sexuality constitute, for *L.A. Law,* the rebellion's most important victims.

FIGURE 3.4. Black leadership? Mayor Tom Bradley.

In *L.A. Law*'s imagination of the uprising, there are no black or latino victims, and there is no black or latino leadership. Indeed, this episode represents repeatedly the corruption or irrelevance of African American public officials. It highlights Tom Bradley's dissociated mumbling about calling in the national guard (fig. 3.4) and it is at pains to remind us of the black district attorney who is indirectly responsible for Zoë's brush with death. This tendency finds its fullest expression in Jonathan Rollins's sham bid to represent South Central in Los Angeles's city council, when, as he tells Leland sheepishly, "Everyone knows I live in Brentwood, just have a post office box in South Central." Even when Jonathan finally drives to "the riot zone" and dispenses with his African American campaign manager, who imagines this trip as nothing more than a photo opportunity, his redemption is assured only by his staying to help a *white* property owner in a futile effort to douse his burning building with a garden hose (fig. 3.5).

FIGURE 3.5. Black leadership? Jonathan Rollins.

Liveness, which is everywhere in this episode, authorizes this revisionist representation of the uprising. The presence and content of live broadcasts within this narrative are constantly adduced as evidence of the crisis-state in which these white Angelenos find themselves. Rather than interrogating the universalizing gaze of liveness, *L.A. Law* does its best to collate that gaze with its own, as in the helicopter-like high-angle shot of Stuart lying beaten next to his car. Worse, it works unceasingly to align our gaze as viewers with liveness's gaze, the gaze that situates us all, like the Simi Valley jury, as frightened suburbanites, all on one side of the thin blue line.

DOOGIE HOWSER, M.D., AND TELEVISUAL INSTRUCTION

The 1992 season premiere of *Doogie Howser* also sustains an extensive dialogue with liveness, foregrounding television sets broadcasting "live" news coverage throughout its mise-en-scène. But the first time we see a television in this program, no one is watching it at all. In the teaser, Doogie, his best friend Vinnie Delpino, and Doogie's parents are gathered in the Howsers' kitchen. Vinnie is trying to convince the senior Dr. Howser to "invest" in the "classic" Nash Rambler that he's trying to raise the money to buy, because such investments are particularly important, he claims, in "these troubled economic times." (Vinnie, the site of endless jokes about the adolescent male libido, is interested in the car because the back seat folds down into a bed.) Doogie's father replies that, on the contrary, he has "a very mature portfolio" and thus "no need to invest in a mobile bedroom." This exchange continues the generational banter about bourgeois masculinity and masculine sexuality that is one of the more persistent preoccupations of the series, even as it reminds the audience of the class status of Doogie's family, which will later become implicated as an explanation for Doogie's particular view of the "riots." Indeed, the teaser connects the "problem" of white male heterosexuality, to which I will return, to the problems posed not only by the rebellion, but also by the project of representing the rebellion on television: after the group disperses, the TV announces to the empty room that "we interrupt our programming to go live to Simi Valley, where the jury has reached a verdict in the Rodney King case" (fig. 3.6).

With its pointedly-unanchored deictic, "we," this televisual proclamation comments uneasily and ironically on what Stephen Heath has called television's "universalization of the function of reception." "Television," he writes, "exists first and foremost as availability, as saying everything to everyone, all of us receivers, assembled and serialized in that unity."[16] But unlike *L.A. Law*, *Doogie Howser* knows, at least, that

FIGURE 3.6. *Doogie Howser*'s unwatched television.

one lesson taught by the uprisings, perhaps *the* lesson, is the impossibility of such unity or universalization of reception: not all of us can embody the helicopters-eye-view, the view of the police. Chiefly through the figure of Raymond, the black former gang member whom Doogie has befriended and rehabilitated as a hospital orderly, this episode registers—however problematically or self-servingly—that, as Doogie remarks, "the bell tolls a little louder for some of us than for others." Or, as Raymond puts it more prosaically, Doogie doesn't, during the rioting, "have to run to a pay phone to see if it's [his] home that's on fire." But *Doogie Howser*'s critique of liveness, signaled initially by this hostile fantasy of the unwatched live broadcast, is energized by more than its suspicion of liveness's claim to produce the unified gaze of the nation. This critique aims ultimately to replace universalized reception with scenes of instruction, and to position fictional TV as the most crucial pedagogical technology for explaining race and history.

The episode works out most of these questions via the figure of Vinnie, who aspires to be a filmmaker and who, expanding on a longstanding trope of the show, arrives in the emergency room after the verdict (he and Doogie have planned to test-drive the Rambler that afternoon) with his video camera and proceeds to get in everyone's way as he pursues his art. Dr. Canfield, Doogie's boss, launches the first assault on Vinnie's vocation and his camera. "Delpino, what are you doing here?" he demands. Vinnie replies "I'm recording history," to which Canfield responds "Do it somewhere else," as he wrenches the camcorder from Vinnie. Undeterred, Vinnie hunts down Doogie, who is treating a fire fighter who's been hit on the head with a brick (fig. 3.7). At this point, a group of small, mostly African American children arrives. Their daycare teacher has been burned trying to put out a fire in her school, and they need looking after while she gets treatment. Doogie, eager to find

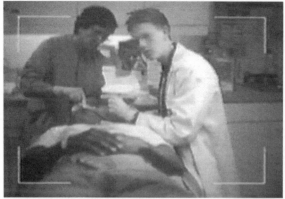

FIGURE 3.7. Vinnie tapes Doogie caring for a patient.

something to take Vinnie out of the emergency room, tells him to take the kids to the pediatric lounge. In a reply crucially evocative of slavery, Vinnie tells Doogie, "I'm an auteur, not a wet nurse." Doogie loses his patience: "Vinnie, *look around*." Here the episode cuts to a point of view shot as Vinnie scans the emergency room. He reluctantly takes the children upstairs.

This entire exchange, with the exception of the final shot from Vinnie's point of view, takes place as he is taping. Thus it seems that the video camera itself prevents Vinnie from seeing what is so obviously going on around him. Indeed, Canfield and Doogie's reactions gesture toward a powerful indictment of amateur video's capacity to see precisely what it purports to see. Furthermore, undermining the credibility of Vinnie's vision also discredits that of George Holliday, and of anyone else who would claim that his tape might be taken as self-evident. The episode thus refuses, albeit obliquely, to indict the Simi Valley jury for the drastic difference between its reading of the Holliday video and that produced by many of those who saw the tape in a different context, embedded in the flow of television news programming. In the process, it interrogates the presumptions that shore up the very live coverage it so voraciously cannibalizes: exhibiting a powerful distrust of video's allegedly privileged relation to immediacy, presence, and the real, *Doogie Howser* puts *its* stock in fictional television's representations, situating them as a better route to cultural understanding, both historically and in the contemporary everyday.

The show tips its hand, revealing its investments in fictional TV's mediation of the shocks of live catastrophe coverage, in a sequence in which Vinnie tries to manage his unruly charges. Here *Doogie Howser* sets up richly condensed relations between race and televisual pedagogy, imagined as a way for white men simultaneously to retain and share power. As a result, this scene is usefully emblematic of the larger project of this episode (and, arguably, the series as a whole) in providing a textual space in which white masculinity tries to renegotiate its own hegemony, sometimes absorbing and containing, sometimes yielding to, real or imagined "threats"—material, representational, and sexual. The sequence opens with an unsteady, clearly hand-held point of view shot from the viewfinder of Vinnie's camcorder, but since it is of Vinnie himself, reading *The Cat in the Hat*, the shot is immediately and unequivocally identified as the enunciation of one of the children (fig. 3.8). The viewfinder shots continue as Vinnie looks up from the book, sees the child, and heads over to retrieve the camera, saying, "Hey, put that down. That's not a toy, kid, that's my life." As Vinnie and the child wrestle for the camera—a struggle evidenced by a wildly unstable image, still from the point of view of the viewfinder—Vinnie intones, "I'm not a violent person, but I've got a copy of *Cat in the Hat* and I'm not afraid to use it," and an off-screen child's voice says, "Oh, I'm really scared." At this point, there's a cut from the viewfinder point-of-view

FIGURE 3.8. One of the children turns the camera on Vinnie.

shot back to the more standard visual discourse of *Doogie Howser*: a medium shot of Vinnie, having retrieved the camcorder, walking across the lounge to try to dissuade another of the African American children from "playing" with the fire alarm. "Look, that's not a toy either," Vinnie says, "The toys are the brightly colored plastic things around here. Here, why don't you play with this fairy magic wand?" The children scream with laughter as the little boy hits Vinnie over the head with the wand.

If we understand the struggle over the camcorder in the opening of this sequence as related to the first struggle with Canfield and to Doogie's derisive "Vinnie, *look around*," the potentially disruptive appropriation of the enunciative powers of video technology by a child of color here is always already undermined. Vinnie's words, "Put that down, that's not a toy," serve only to call attention to the fact that his camcorder has been "proven" by the episode to be just that—an annoying disruption to the real, immediate, embodied work of the hospital staff. The persistent dismissal of the possibility of camcorder activism is rendered all the more striking by the fact that the episode, most centrally concerned with the damage done to persons and property by fire, hints at the stakes of such representational appropriation by aligning the video camera with the fire alarm, which fascinates one of these children but which is "not a toy either." This show thus suggests that redistributing control over media representation might be an alternative way of putting out some urban fires. The show does no such thing, however, for the implications of this moment are thoroughly contained by conventions of TV comedy: "playing" with the video camera or the fire alarm is inappropriate in the same way that it's inappropriate for a child to hit Vinnie with the "fairy magic wand."

What should we make of the interruption of this scene by the word "fairy," which is, of course, completely unnecessary to describe this object? Ideologically, Vinnie's offer of the "fairy magic wand" embeds both a utopian promise and a rebuke. On one hand, it's an appropriate toy, unlike the camcorder and the fire alarm, and its magic might transcend the thoroughly material work that the nontoys can perform. On the other, the "fairy-ness" of the wand is unstable, always threatening to transfer itself to its bearer and emasculate him. Thus we might guess that when the boy hits Vinnie over the head with the wand, he is trying to transfer its effeminizing potential back onto Vinnie. The mock-violence of the exchange of the wand between Vinnie and the boy thus mobilizes the threats—instabilities of racial, sexual, and hegemonic positions—that white heterosexual masculinity in general, and *Doogie Howser* in particular, must work to manage. Thus, in the context of *Doogie Howser*'s obsession with documenting the vicissitudes of suburban white adolescent male heterosexuality (the series' attention to sexuality is indeed this precise), the exchange of the fairy magic wand condenses several of the "others" of the sexual position that the show likes to imagine for its main characters, others which are nonetheless always present in the show's production of Doogie and Vinnie's sexual subjectivity: African American male sexuality (elsewhere centered in the presence of Raymond), the sexuality of children (elsewhere located in the original boy-in-a-man's-world premise of the show), and gay sexuality (elsewhere and everywhere present within the abiding homosocial bond between Vinnie and Doogie).

That such condensation—particularly of black male sexuality and gay male sexuality as threats to white bourgeois masculinity—might find its way into an episode on Rodney King should not surprise us. As Butler has pointed out, the sexual iconography of the Holliday video—"the image of the police standing over Rodney King with their batons"—evokes "a punishment for [King's] conjectured or desired sexual aggression" (21). Part of the work the fairy magic wand does in this scene, then, is to invoke King and his beating, to stand in for the police batons whose "fairy-ness" is also shifting, unstable in relation to the "sexual aggression" that is widely and popularly assumed to reside in black men, and that is persistently conjectured or desired as containing within it the capacity to interpellate white men as its objects. As in the beating itself, the intensity of the sexualized aggression in the exchange of the wand threatens to undermine the stability of white masculinity: if Vinnie begins this encounter in the position of the police, purporting to respond to the child's unruliness with the violently gratuitous and contaminating deployment of the word "fairy," the child is able to appropriate that position and hit back. In this way, the scene, as a fantasized reenactment of the beating, restages the "logic" of the Simi Valley jurors who imagined King to be "in complete control," and clarifies the intertwined roles racism and homophobia played in the production of the jury's reading of the video.

In the closing moments of the sequence, this collation of sexuality, race, and the televisual negotiations of white male hegemony meets up explicitly with *Doogie Howser*'s critique of liveness and its claims for the pedagogic potential of fictional television. Vinnie's solution to the magic wand problem is to turn on the television, forgetting that one of the markers of catastrophe is that one finds the same thing on every channel (fig. 3.9). Liveness—in this case, images of fire—generates questions that only fictional television can answer: faced with the children's queries about what they've seen, Vinnie seeks to instruct them on race relations by promising to tell them "the whole thing": "It all started with this guy called Rodney King . . . You know what? I'm going to

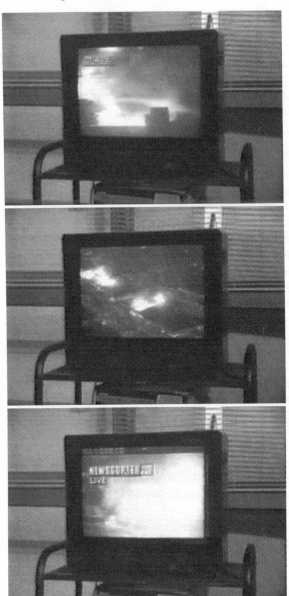

FIGURE 3.9.
Catastrophe
coverage: the same
thing on every
channel.

have go back further than this." Blank looks from the children. "Martin
Luther King." Another blank look. He pulls up a chair, looks at them
earnestly, and says, "Once upon a time there was this guy called Kunta
Kinte" — blank looks — "who came to America on Ed Asner's slave ship."

Vinnie's reference to *Roots* returns us to his remark to Doogie earlier in the episode that he is "an auteur, not a wet nurse," a remark in which Vinnie wards off the specter of finding himself interpellated as a black woman, but in which the gesture of warding off serves only to situate his own masculinity more firmly as beleaguered, and beleaguered specifically in relation to a complex and volatile reenactment of the scene of slavery organized by a series of mirroring binarisms. In other words, even though Vinnie is a white man, not a black woman, being asked to care for black children rather than white ones, the perfect symmetry of his position relative to that of the wet nurse threatens always to deconstruct his opposition to her. But the invocation of *Roots* undoes the abjection of Vinnie's earlier self-insertion into the narrative of slavery, and thus provisionally secures the ground of white masculinity and heterosexuality: here Vinnie deploys this narrative *not* from the position of the wet nurse; here, at least, he gets to tell the story of slavery from the outside, from a position something like that of the auteur.

And from that of the *lecteur*: Vinnie's lecture — situated in this scene as ridiculous, with the children's blankness played for laughs — is eventually shown to evolve into a productive discussion with at least one of the children about the beating, the verdict, and its aftermath. Fictional television — here, *Roots* specifically — thus turns out to be pedagogically useful by generating a scene of instruction in which the white teacher "explains" the racial history of the United States to six children of color. And through this consideration of pedagogy, these scenes inscribe the series' profound ambivalence about its own situation within the white-liberal culture industry, a situation in which *Doogie Howser* is both acutely aware of the specificity — and thus the limitations — of its privileged access to the airwaves, and is simultaneously completely unwilling to imagine sharing that access. The answer to this dilemma, as *Doogie Howser* imagines it, is for mainstream network television to function didactically in relation to its audiences of color.

But this gesture is itself complicated, in these scenes, by the children's persistent construction as a less than appreciative audience for Vinnie's lesson. Their disaffection echoes the unwatched verdict of the teaser, and returns us to the question of reception that *Doogie Howser* is so worried about: if it rejects the falsely universal national gaze of liveness — a powerful fantasy of mass viewership in those early days of cable's challenge to network hegemony — what might a plausible alternative be? How could *Doogie Howser* find an audience for its lectures? The answer to these questions may lie in the fact that network audiences of the late '80s and early '90s were disproportionately of color, since predominately African American and Latino inner-city neighborhoods were the cable industry's final, and as yet unreached, frontier.

The children in these scenes, and their parents, might plausibly be understood as stand-ins for the actual viewers *Doogie Howser*, and shows like it, needed to address.

RODNEY KING DEAD

"For all its ideology of 'liveness,' it may be death that forms the point of televisual intrigue." In this line from "Information, Crisis, Catastrophe," Mary Ann Doane points out that liveness, as a crucial televisual rhetoric of catastrophe coverage, is always linked with catastrophe TV's primary object: death.[17] Live TV is always haunted by the possibility of death. If we take seriously this linkage between liveness and death, then what are the specters that trouble the texts of King TV? I would like to conclude by proposing two answers to that question. First, as I've suggested in my reading of *Doogie Howser*'s extended meditation on liveness, one ghostly other of live TV is dead TV, or, more specifically, the long, drawn-out death of the major networks, gradually bled of their audiences by cable, satellite, video, and DVD. We can read the enthusiastic deployment of live catastrophe coverage and its fictional recyclings by network television as one of the ways in which the networks attempt continually to reinvent their own relevance to national life. And in this regard, King TV (like Thomas/Hill) was particularly efficacious from the networks' point of view, given their quest, in the late '80s and early '90s, for African American audiences: at that moment in U.S. television's history, there was a particularly pressing market imperative to rehash endlessly the vicissitudes of race in America.

Second, the production and reception of Rodney King Live requires also the invocation and repression of Rodney King Dead. These requirements, I think, lay at the heart of the capacity of King's query — *Can't we all get along?* — to transfix the nation, and also at the heart of the necessity for that query to be so immediately and widely ironized: King's authority at that moment was so eerie because his was, in a sense, a voice from the dead. The power of the Holliday video, after all, lay in its spectacularly awful and thankfully unkept promise finally to catch Darryl Gates's LAPD in the act of beating a black man to death. In this respect, the video, and the wider televisual flow through which it circulated, placed King as a stand-in for the "invisible" or at least unvideotaped black victims of police murder in Los Angeles, and elsewhere: for Eulia Love, say, or Eleanor Bumpers, or Michael Stewart. It is their spirits who lurk at the margins of these texts.

Finally, though, both of these answers are in one way at least the

same answer: network television, scrambling for African American viewers, self-promoting, and sensationalist, found itself telling and re-telling the story of U.S. race relations, and in the process, chronicling the violent eruptions of dreams deferred. Found itself, in other words, fading to black.

Rodney King beading
—live TV / amateur video

CHAPTER FOUR

Giuliani Time: Urban Policing and *Brooklyn South*

IN THIS CHAPTER, as in the last, I examine a collision between televisual representation and the lived history of police brutality in black communities. If my concern in the last chapter was chiefly for the effects of such collisions on television itself, I am more interested here in how intersections between television and the police shape politics and everyday life within contemporary American cities. I focus here on one such crash of the social with the representational, which occurred in 1997: the police assault, in August, on Abner Louima in Brooklyn's 70th precinct house and the premiere, in late September, of a new police drama called *Brooklyn South*.

How can cultural representation aid in the sociopolitical project of abridging civil rights? To put the question another way, how can television help generate and sustain consensus around a set of public policies, in this case Mayor Rudolph Giuliani's law-and-order strategies with respect to policing, which were obviously both unjust and unreasonable?[1] My argument will assume fundamentally that Giuliani's approach to policing makes no sense, whether it is carried out in New York or exported to other cities; whether it is seen from the perspective of an advocacy of equal treatment and equal protection—which clearly held no interest for Giuliani—or from that of efficacious policy or even political self-interest—which clearly held more than a little interest for him. How do large, diverse, and sophisticated populations carry on urban business as usual, as if persuaded that the aggressive defense of indefensible police actions makes sense?

The suggestion that television—and entertainment television at that—plays an important role in the conversion of nonsense to common sense is clearly not a wildly original one. And it would be a serious methodological and political error to elevate the effects of *Brooklyn South* over the ordinarily pervasive structures of racism and classism that go a long way toward explaining Giuliani's success. Nor do I mean to dismiss the importance of lower crime rates in modulating public concern about police brutality and corruption.[2] Nonetheless, I think *Brooklyn South* is worth examining for two reasons. Specifically, the temporal proximity of its premiere to the attack on Louima suggests that the program's narratives may have served as one way in which viewers processed, both psychically and politically, the assault and its aftershocks. The text of *Brooklyn South*, as I will demonstrate, reimagined Louima (or more precisely, the Louima-function, the black man assaulted by police) as a homicidal maniac, and Brooklyn police officers as generally presenting a unified front against police abuse. Such processing of the social through the representational, I suggest, tends to contain the disruptive challenges to police and mayoral authority posed either by the savagery of the officers involved in this particular case, or by the NYPD's generalized and blatant disregard for the civil rights of those whom they are supposed to serve and protect.

Contemporary policing has emerged in the U.S. as a key civil rights battleground, at lease for poor, urban communities of color. If, as Judith Grant has argued, cop shows generally "favor force over rules as ways to resolve conflict," any extended consideration of contemporary policing must take such programs into account as a key ideological technology in moving civil rights struggles out of federal courts and into precinct houses and interrogation rooms.[3] Indeed, I would suggest that the proliferation of cop shows might be read as one of the ways in which television has responded to and extended the national fetishization of "law and order" in post-1968 American culture, a fetishization that has been crucial to the conservative reimagination of movements for civil rights, which has taken place during the same period. If the cop show in general is a machine that produces disciplined, lawful subjects whose primary point of entry into narratives about crime will be their identification with the police, *Brooklyn South* is a preeminently efficient machine indeed. As I hope to demonstrate, all of the elements of *Brooklyn South*'s text — its narrative structure, its camera work and editing, its use of sound — are finely calibrated to encourage this identification.[4]

GIULIANI TIME

Coproduced by Steven Bochco and CBS, *Brooklyn South* is set in Brooklyn's 74th Precinct. Reviewers have noted its envelope-pushing realism: the first nine minutes of the pilot episode — which I will discuss at length a bit later — were unprecedentedly violent, making *Brooklyn South* an instant poster-child for the then just-introduced television ratings system. In addition, the "cop talk" is so thickly "authentic" that the dialogue, and thus the plots, in the first few episodes were extremely hard to follow. (CBS actually provided a glossary on the show's web page.) Well before the pilot aired on September 22, though, industry watchers in the popular press were struck by further evidence of the show's "authenticity": the fact that the first few episodes of the series dealt with the death, in the station house, of a black suspect in police custody.[5]

Parallels to the Louima case were drawn immediately. Abner Louima was arrested in a contretemps with police outside a Haitian club in Flatbush, where his favorite singer was performing. He was beaten, he claims, on the way to the station, by four officers of the 70th precinct. When he arrived at the station, he was taken into the precinct bathroom, where he was sodomized by one of the officers, Justin Volpe, with the wooden handle of a mop.[6] Volpe then forced the handle into his mouth. Police then declined for ninety minutes to provide a police escort to the ambulance that arrived to take Louima, with life-threatening injuries to his colon and bladder, to the hospital; when he finally got there, he was held under guard, handcuffed to his bed, and denied visitors.[7] Officers explained his injuries by saying they had been sustained in a homosexual encounter. After he was treated, a hospital worker reported the incident in a phone call to the Internal Affairs Bureau, a call that was neither logged nor followed up. Relatives of Louima who went to the precinct to file a complaint were told to "go home."[8]

In public discourse, the assault on Abner Louima was immediately temporalized, linked to the particular period of Rudolph Giuliani's mayoral administration. Immediately after the attack Louima claimed that his assailant had admonished him during the beating to respect the police because "this is Giuliani time, not Dinkins time."[9] Louima later recanted this reference to New York City's current and former mayors, and testified at the officers' trial that "he had begun falsely reporting it at the urging of a supporter—a brother-in-law of a nurse at Coney Island Hospital, where he was then being treated—who told him that he was an auxiliary police officer and frequently heard police officers make such statements."[10] But whether or not the slogan represented authentic evidence of the internal culture of the NYPD, the fact remains that the phrase "Giuliani Time" proved for many New Yorkers a durable and evocative descriptor of the meeting point of politics and everyday life during the city's late-1990s "boom."[11]

It is impossible to understand the events in the Louima case without considering more broadly the urban temporality of Giuliani Time. Giuliani Time was a fantastical temporality, energized by a vision of the city with a Starbucks on every corner, Gap-ified, Disney-fied, and washed clean of undesirable elements like public sex and poor people. Indeed, in a moment refreshing in its candor, a top Giuliani aide looked forward to the day when New York's poor would simply *leave the city* because they realized that it's better to be homeless in warmer climates.[12] The capital of this imaginary New York, of course, was the "new" Times Square.[13]

Most often, Giuliani Time was marked out by battles in a low-intensity war between the mayor and the unruly masses of New Yorkers who continually and frustratingly refused to conduct themselves according to his desires. During his tenure, Giuliani engaged in well-publicized skirmishes with midtown pedestrians, city cabbies, local hot dog vendors, and, perhaps most famously, the Brooklyn Museum. But the mayor was not content to reserve his efforts to micromanaging everyday life: in addition to his sustained economic and social assault on the city's poor (via welfare "reform" and new policies on homelessness) and on sexual subcultures, Giuliani showered public resources and mayoral approbation on a police force that seemed to many to be spinning dangerously out of control.

In Giuliani Time, "safety" was paramount, and, indeed, the overall crime rate in New York dropped significantly.[14] But it was a particular kind of safety, designed for a particular class of persons, and purchased at a high price: as Samuel Delaney noted recently, the person for whom the new Times Square was supposed to be safe was the middle-class tourist from the suburbs.[15] Other kinds of persons, though, found ourselves dramatically *less* safe. In Giuliani Time, under the mayor's celebrated "zero tolerance" policies, entire classes of persons—"squeegee guys," youth of color, sex workers, and the poor—were effectively criminalized as the agents of what Giuliani's administration dubbed "quality of life" offenses. As a result, charges of police brutality and misconduct increased significantly relative to the final year of the Dinkins administration, and a vastly disproportionate number of the victims of police abuses were people of color.[16] In Giuliani Time, as Amnesty International reported in a 1996 study, "it is rare for NYPD officers to be criminally prosecuted for on-duty excessive force and even rarer for convictions to be obtained."[17] In Giuliani Time, the City of New York spent just over $29 million dollars settling cases of police abuse in 1997 alone, and by the end of 1997 the city had spent a total of $98 million dollars settling them since Giuliani had taken office.[18] In Giuliani Time, many of the debates about the mayor's stewardship of the department have revolved around the question of how best to "police the police," and more particularly around the question of independent monitoring of cases of abuse and corruption. A short history of those debates during Giuliani's first term will provide a context for the rest of my discussion.

On March 27, 1998, a *New York Times* front-page headline announced "Giuliani Dismisses Police Proposals by His Task Force," while a subhead noted "Mayor's Tone is Caustic." The accompanying article detailed the latest phase in New York Mayor Rudolph Giuliani's ongoing resistance to police reform, noting that he had greeted the report of his own "Task Force on Police and Community Relations" with "insult" and "sarcasm," and dismissed most of its recommendations.[19] The *Times*'s subhead echoed, for followers of Mr. Giuliani's bizarre approach to public relations, countless earlier headlines for stories specifying the mayor's penchant for treating those with whom he disagrees with a combination of arrogance and petulance. More crucially, the headline echoed, for followers of the Giuliani administration's relations with the New York Police Department, countless earlier titles for stories elaborating the mayor's repudiation of proposals made by the Mollen Commission to Investigate Police Corruption, the New York City Council, and, occasionally, police department insiders.

The Mollen Commission was appointed in 1992 by Giuliani's predecessor, David Dinkins, after Michael Dowd, a Brooklyn cop, was arrested by Suffolk County police on drug charges.[20] After a two-year investigation, the commission's final report documented that, in certain black and Hispanic neighborhoods, groups of rogue cops had organized into criminal "crews" much like street gangs and were dealing drugs, using departmental equipment in break-ins, skimming cash recovered from crime scenes, and "terrorizing" residents.[21] The report also identified what it called "willful blindness" to corruption pervasive among precinct commanders and departmental investigators, reluctance on the part of honest officers to report corrupt colleagues, willingness on the part of police union officials to tip off cops under investigation, and resistance to investigating corrupt cops for fear that negative publicity might be damaging to the department's reputation.[22]

The commission proposed a number of strategies to reduce police corruption, including raising the minimum age of recruits from 20 to 22, increasing random drug testing, and expanding Internal Affairs' use of undercover agents.[23] But debates about the commission's recommendations quickly crystallized around the question of how to police the police. The commission, citing what Chairman Milton Mollen called "the shocking . . . incompetence and inadequacy of the police department to police itself," called for the creation of an independent "Police Commission" with investigative and subpoena power.[24] Giuliani, who was elected to his first term as mayor in 1993—thanks, in part, to the endorsement of the Patrolmen's Benevolent Association—was faced with the task of reconciling the commission's endorsement of a monitoring body with the resistance of various sectors of law enforcement. He managed this assignment with an aplomb both admirable and alarming, claiming consistently for several years both to support external oversight of the force while engineering just as consistently the impossibility of such oversight.

Immediately after his election, for example, Giuliani stated that he supported the establishment of a special prosecutor's office to investigate charges of corruption and brutality, rather than the five-member panel recommended by the commission.[25] A casual observer might at the time have reasonably accepted the mayor-elect's claim that such an entity would be "even more independent" and thus even more effective in combating police malfeasance.[26] But a clue to the fact that Giuliani might not have been telling the whole story was provided soon after the election by the *New York Times*: "Last week, aides to Mr. Giuliani, who spoke only on the condition of anonymity, said it was unlikely that he would fully accept the proposals of a commission that in effect is a lame-duck group appointed by a lame-duck Mayor."[27] And a closer examination of Giuliani's proposal reveals a crucial loophole. As *Newsday* reported on November 19, 1993, "Commission members were also troubled when Giuliani publicly recommended the formation of a special prosecutor's office to fight police wrongdoing. Although the commission hasn't yet issued its final proposal, a special prosecutor's office is considered a dead issue because Gov. Mario Cuomo's top law-enforcement officials say the state won't pay for it."[28] Indeed, Giuliani continued to champion the idea of a special prosecutor until August 1994, just two-and-a-half months before Cuomo was defeated by George Pataki.[29]

At the same time, though, during the period from April through August 1994, the administration continued to float other proposals. At the end of April, *Newsday* quoted a Giuliani aide as saying that the mayor "has been extremely supportive of the commission, even backing off his campaign endorsement of a special state prosecutor to investigate police corruption until he hears what type of independent oversight the commission will recommend."[30] The next day, *Newsday* reported that the mayor was waffling on the question of whether the group would have "the power to conduct its own investigations," a power that was a crucial element of the Mollen recommendation.[31] Nine weeks later, after the commission released its final report, the *Times* reported that "in recent months, [the mayor] has indicated that he leans toward giving the outside monitoring powers to the city's Department of Investigation," which is charged with monitoring public corruption city-wide, rather than to a group dedicated specifically to investigating police.[32]

Finally, on August 20, the *Times* related that "Mayor Giuliani said for the first time that he favored creating an independent agency to monitor corruption in New York City's Police Department, and he said he would try to reach agreement with the City Council on what powers to give it."[33] The same day, *Newsday* noted that "Giuliani said he wants the panel to be created by the City Council rather than by a mayoral executive order." When the City Council passed a bill that did just that, by a vote of 39 to 9 in October, Giuliani immediately announced his plans to veto the bill, claiming that the council had arrogated to itself powers properly belonging to the mayor, and objecting to the council's plan that the panel have subpoena and investigative powers.[34] The veto finally came in December; when the Council overrode the veto a month later, the mayor replied that he would "ignore" the vote. In February 1995, as Internal Affairs was uncovering a major corruption scandal in the Bronx's 48th Precinct (which eventually resulted in the indictment of sixteen of the precinct's officers) he announced plans to create his own panel by executive order.[35] The mayor's panel would be appointed entirely by Giuliani, and would have investigative and subpoena power to be used only at his discretion (or, in the *Times*'s words, "at the Mayor's pleasure").[36] By the end of the month, Giuliani's panel was in place, and the mayor was threatening to sue the City Council "within a week if Speaker Peter Vallone (D-Queens) does not agree on a new format giving the mayor power to appoint all commission members."[37] The mayor filed this suit in April.

In June, while the courts adjudicated the mayor's conflict with the council, the debate over police monitoring shifted. Members of the NYPD, in Washington to attend a memorial for slain police officers, went on a drunken rampage in their hotels. Officers, "some in uniform and some naked, groped at women, shot off fire extinguishers and caused extensive damage in hotel corridors."[38] In the wake of this scandal, Giuliani announced sweeping new anticorruption measures. In the process, he appropriated many of the Mollen Commission's recommendations for his own political gain, even as he shifted the burden of investigating charges against police from the Internal Affairs Bureau to individual precinct commanders.[39] At the end of the month, State Supreme Court Justice Beatrice Shainswit ruled with Giuliani that the City Council "overstepped its authority" in creating the police monitoring panel.[40]

In less than two years, in other words, Giuliani had managed to turn oversight (a term whose double sense I invoke advisedly) of the police over to the department itself, all the while claiming that he supported independent superintendence of the force. It is shocking, though hardly surprising, then, that Giuliani's panel, the "Commission to Combat Police Corruption," issued its first report praising "significant improvements in the New York City Police Department's anti-corruption efforts," or that the *Times* eventually reported that "a meddling City Hall and an uncooperative Police Department have rendered [the mayor's panel] largely irrelevant."[41]

So determined was the mayor's resistance to independent police review that the struggle between the City Council and the mayor's office over police monitoring was reenacted almost to the letter in the wake of the Louima scandal. In a chain of events beginning in September 1997, the City Council again tried to create an independent police review board in revised legislation that granted the mayor the right to approve all the board's members. Giuliani again vetoed the council's proposal, the council again overrode the veto, and the mayor again sued the council to block formation of the board.[42] This time, though, the suit was unsuccessful, although the mayor's office vowed to appeal State Supreme Court Justice Richard F. Braun's ruling. The outrageousness of the mayor's opposition to police review, given the excesses of the Louima case, was neatly smoke-screened by the administration's grudging concession, in mid-September, to increase the budget of the city's Civilian Complaint Review Board — the drastically under-funded ninety-eight pound weakling of NYPD oversight — by a measly $1.5 million.[43]

Giuliani's opposition to any genuinely independent entity empowered to investigate — much less to discipline — criminal officers of the New York Police Department thus persisted through outside investigations by Amnesty International and the federal government. It endured numerous department scandals involving corruption and brutality, unwavering in the wake of the assault on Abner Louima, the shooting of Amadou Diallo, and the shooting of Gidone Busch, to name only the best-publicized recent incidents. It persevered as the city's costs to settle lawsuits against the department skyrocketed.

But the costs of Giuliani's consistency and the police abuse that accompanied it were garnered not only from the city budget, of course, but from the bodies and spirits of its citizens. This price is often extracted as the commission paid in the conversion of different denominations of masculine capital. In other words, the circulation of particular masculinities through historically and racially specific communities frequently requires the extraction of these surcharges in the form, too often, of literal pounds of flesh from racially or sexually Othered bodies. It is as if majoritarian culture, noting the Othered body's superabundance to the rationally disembodied public sphere, tries violently to cut it to size.[44] I will track these exchanges through a set of representations depicting white police officers in brutal transactions with their others. On, then, to the fortunes of race and sexuality as currencies in a ruthless marketplace of identity, *Brooklyn South*.

How to Identify with the Cops

Given its appearance during Giuliani Time, just weeks before Giuliani's victory over Ruth Messinger for a second term, it is crucial to specify *Brooklyn South*'s central ideological project: to encourage its audience's identification with the police, to locate its viewers inside the "house" (the police station) and not as members of either "the community" —

which the show depicts as violent, foolish, and irrational—or the Internal Affairs Bureau—which the show depicts as predatory and overzealous. The extent to which the series will go in this regard was borne out paratextually by its official CBS-sponsored web page. Visitors were granted entry to the site by answering correctly one of the questions on the New York Police Academy entrance exam. Once admitted, they found, along with the standard cast bios and episode summaries, an audio link allowing them to listen "live" to Brooklyn police scanners; an up-to-date listing, complete with photos and vital statistics, race prominent among them, of "Brooklyn's [real life] Most Wanted"; and the aforementioned "Cop Talk" glossary.

On a number of levels, the text of *Brooklyn South* is itself structured to encourage identification with its protagonists by providing us with ample scenes of their private lives, immersing us in police-procedural details, and granting us privileged access to the inner sancta of police life: locker rooms, interrogation rooms, "cop bars," and the like. These elements of the series are unsurprising. More remarkable, though, are the lengths to which the series goes to foreclose spectators' resistant, oppositional, or disidentificatory readings.

In this way, the series is a marked departure from the currently dominant conventions for prime-time drama, conventions Bochco himself pioneered in series like *Hill Street Blues* and *L.A. Law*. These series, and most of the dramatic series that followed them, are carefully organized to maximize ratings by allowing multiple—and sometimes conflicting—possibilities for viewer engagement across political, economic, and social locations. Such organization has proved particularly useful for shows dealing with controversial contemporary issues; with their shared ripped-from-the-headlines aesthetic, *Brooklyn South*'s contemporaries in the police procedural genre (like *NYPD Blue*, *Law and Order*, and *Homicide: Life on the Street*), are meticulous in offering their viewers a number of positions on such issues by building them into characterization or narrative structure.[45] Unlike its generic cohort, then, *Brooklyn South* actively works to render the viewer's engagement with the white male officers' various Others at least unappealing and at worst actively dangerous. In this respect, the show's ideological project may have actually subverted its commercial one: *Brooklyn South*'s refusal to offer multiple identificatory inroads for its viewers certainly contributed to its cancellation early in 1998.[46]

The opening of the series' pilot episode provides a concise example of how *Brooklyn South* deploys narrative and visual elements to structure viewer identification. Critics who reviewed the pilot focused on the considerable violence, extreme even for its genre, that earned this episode television's first "TV-MA" rating (mature audiences). I am interested less in the fact of the violence, though, than in the ways that violence is organized and rendered systematic by the sequence's editing.

The sequence opens with a minor car accident between a retired cop and the Asian woman who rear-ends him. Marking the Brooklyn street-scape as one organized, if not riven, by racial conflict, the former cop accuses the woman of "driving while Oriental." When she refuses to leave her car, he flags down two uniformed officers, telling them that the woman is behaving "as though I'm after her for Pearl Harbor or something." Meanwhile, back at the station, officers in roll call are being briefed on conditions in the precinct. Patrol Sergeant Frank Donovan (Jon Tenney) alerts his officers to be on the lookout for "this ass-hole, Deshawn Hopkins" (fig. 4.1) as he points to a picture of a black man plastered to the front of the podium behind which he is speaking. A cut takes us back out the street, where we see Hopkins, unprovoked, punching a white man on the street, then kicking in the headlight of a passing car before coming up behind one of the officers involved in the traffic stop and shooting him, execution style, in the back of the head. During the next six minutes, Hopkins continues to kill police officers, despite being shot several times himself, until he is finally apprehended by Officer Jimmy Doyle (Dylan Walsh) and brought into custody.

There are a couple of remarkable things about the editing of this sequence, in that it breaks two rules generally held dear by television editors: it contains two jump cuts and at least two significant continuity errors. In both cases, these transgressions of standard television editing practices are thematically linked. A jump cut joins two shots in which the camera in the second shot is positioned less than 30 degrees away from where it was positioned in the first shot; because the camera positions for the two shots are so close together, the shots look very similar. Thus the jump cut has the effect of repeating the image with only a slight difference. Editors of U.S. commercial television generally avoid jump cuts because they are considered overly obtrusive, calling attention to the editing itself rather than the content of the two shots joined by the cut. In *Brooklyn South*, both jump cuts join two shots of cops leaving the safety of their cars to engage Hopkins; they thus double and insist on the counterintuitive and courageous determination of the officers to enter the fray.

Continuity errors are violations of the system of editing, perfected by Hollywood and inherited by television, designed to minimize the disruption of the cut in favor of maintaining continuous narrative action by matching the direction, movement, and position of figures from shot to shot. The continuity errors in the sequence I've described have to do with the perpetrator, Hopkins, and the virtually magical appearances of his guns. There is a moment as Hopkins is described on the soundtrack

FIGURE 4.1. "This asshole, Deshawn Hopkins."

as a cocaine addict, just after he slugs the innocent bystander who has the misfortune to bump into him, which suggests that Hopkins has a gun tucked into the front of his pants, under his sweatshirt. The appearance of a gun held behind his back seven shots later is thus difficult to explain, given that the editor seems to have passed up an opportunity to build suspense by displaying Hopkins readying his weapon. When, later in this sequence Hopkins suddenly appears and begins firing *two* guns where before he had only one, these rhyming narrative omissions — the text's refusal to explain where these guns come from — seem self-conscious enough (or perhaps *un*-self-conscious enough) to establish *Brooklyn South*'s insistence on Hopkins's virtually supernatural powers. With his maniacal-yet-glazed expression and uncanny calm, Hopkins seems able to conjure weapons from nowhere.

If this sequence is willing to flout some of the conventions of realist editing, though, it is also scrupulous in its observation of other such conventions, notably the manipulation of point of view in the production of viewer identification. In particular, the editing here is extremely careful to align the spectator's view of what transpires with that of the police. Hopkins is given only one point-of-view shot in the entire sequence; the police are clearly assigned at least six. In addition, certain key shots that are not assigned to individual characters' POV are allied with the gaze of police. Consider, for example, the mug shot to which Donovan gestures at roll call, and which serves as a kind of establishing shot for what follows. Or the overhead shot of the slain body of the first officer Hopkins shoots (fig. 4.2). While this shot was most likely made with a crane, the extreme high angle suggests another trope of contemporary police narrative: the surveilling view from a police helicopter that I discuss in chapter 3 (compare fig. 3.3).

FIGURE 4.2. Cops-eye-view.

FIGURE 4.3.
Hopkins takes aim.

But if the cops are afforded, directly or indirectly, much of the power of the controlling gaze here, the tension in the sequence is produced by the menacing gaze of Hopkins, frequently represented as coterminous with his magically lethal firearms. Hopkins *looks* in order to *take aim* (fig. 4.3). And the sequence deliberately confuses the question of at whom Hopkins is aiming, painstakingly conflating its spectators' position with that of the police/victims by the astonishing number of shots (twelve) that depict Hopkins moving menacingly or actually firing directly toward the camera. The spectator of this sequence, then, is carefully located in such a way as to experience both the police officer's power and his vulnerability.

Both textually and paratextually, then, *Brooklyn South* participates in the "us vs. them" epistemology of Giuliani Time and, in the process, does its best to align its audience with the racism and classism that currently organize the nation's most important urban spaces. Clearly the series understands this "us" to be white and male, despite the token inclusion, among *Brooklyn South*'s characters, of two women officers (one white, one African American) and a male Latino officer. Indeed, the series' algebraic arrangement of racial and sexual difference renders the terms "police," "white," and "male" equivalent to one another in such a way as to make women and Latinos irrelevant, and male African American cops impossible. This tendency allowed a miscalculation simultaneously bizarre and utterly predictable: as originally cast, the show included no black male officers. Indeed, the entire pilot was reshot during the summer of 1997 after producer David Milch "noticed" that this omission might imply "a racial statement which was utterly unintended, a sense of 'us vs. them.' "[47] He went on to note "the paradox is, I didn't think in racial categories, which, of course, is the ultimate goal of our society."[48]

GOOD COP, BAD COP

Brooklyn South bifurcates the Louima incident into two separate plot lines, one involving the death of Hopkins in police custody and one involving a gay-bashing by cops. With the verb "bifurcates," I am not claiming that the producers of the series intended explicitly to rewrite the Louima narrative in the particular ways that they did (we know that at least the pilot was in the can before the attack on Louima). I am instead pointing out the temporal coexistence of these narratives within a larger social discourse about race and policing, and insisting that these narratives function within those discourses as at least mutually inflecting, facilitating the conscious and unconscious identifications with the police that I've argued are crucial to the smooth functioning of the ideological discourses of law and order.

To pick up the first plot after the clip I've described, Hopkins is dragged into the station house, where some of the surviving officers briefly consider leaving him where he can't get medical attention. He then dies, to the satisfaction of several of the cops. Internal Affairs, however, isn't so satisfied. Armed with an autopsy report saying that Hopkins died of a punctured lung from compression fractures to the chest, and that he sustained these injuries "after he was in the house," IAB Lieutenant Sam Jonas (James B. Sikking) commences investigating the issue of how the police "comported themselves" during the incident, causing Donovan to remark bitterly "Psycho killing people on the streets and they'll look to make us wrong."

As the story unfolds over several episodes, complete with unreasonable and overzealous African American community leaders holding premature rallies and press conferences, the IAB investigation focuses on Officer Jack Lowery (Titus Welliver), who was seen to slap Hopkins while subduing him. The audience, however, knows that the real culprit may be Officer Ann-Marie Kersey (Yancy Butler), whose fiancé, another cop, was killed in the incident and who admits to Donovan that she kicked Hopkins in the back and thus possibly dealt the deadly blow herself. Later, however, after a grand jury refuses to indict Lowery, and Donovan inexplicably persuades Kersey not to come forward, all is forgiven when the Medical Examiner issues yet another report saying that Hopkins died of his gunshot wounds after all.

The second brutality plot line appears in episode seven, "Love Hurts," in which officers are called to the scene of a fight between two white men outside a gay bar. They find an enraged older man beating his passive and pathetic lover, claiming he has made a pass at another man, a black man. The cuckolded lover (who has quite a mouth on him) calls this figure "Paul Robeson" and "Jackie Robinson," but he actually serves as a figure for Abner Louima, who was, after all, arrested outside a club in which, according at least to his assailants, abusive gay sex took place. Into the breach of this mélange of conflicting masculine styles — straight machismo, butch gay male, snap queen, gay milquetoast — series regulars Officers Roussakoff (Michael DeLuise) and Villanueva (Adam Rodriguez) leap to take the batterer into custody. But when Roussakoff is hit in the head with a bottle and needs Villanueva to take him to the hospital, they hand off the arrest to two episodic characters, Officers Heagan and Pitterino. Suspicions are roused immediately at the precinct when Heagan and Pitterino arrive with the men, the older of whom has been badly beaten on the way into the house. They claim that his lover has inflicted the damage; for his part, the lover claims that one of the officers has run his partner's head into a dumpster. During the rest of the episode, the 74th precinct is letter-perfect in its investigation of the brutality charge: Roussakoff and Villanueva serve not as a blue wall of silence but as champions of "the truth"; and another cop, who witnessed the beating while off duty, appears unprompted to give Sergeant Santoro the number of the patrol car driven by the offending officers. The plot winds down with Heagan, who actually administered the beating, vociferously blaming "those fags" for ruining his life before he breaks down in tears asking, "Oh my god, what did I do?"

In Brooklyn's 74th Precinct, then, as opposed to the 70th, police brutality is the product not of a widespread culture of lawlessness among men who reasonably expect not to be punished for criminal activity, but rather the product of grief, extreme stress, or gender trouble; its perpetrators, furthermore, are genuinely *sorry* for what they have done. Investigations into misconduct are ardently pursued by IAB — no missing phone calls here — even when the victims are black cop killers or extremely bitchy queens. Fellow officers (with the singular exception of Donovan's protection of Kersey who is, after all, female and thus relatively harmless) consistently place their commitment to the truth before their commitment to their colleagues. Mistakes are made; highly charged situations sometimes get out of hand, but the disciplinary systems internal to the department are entirely adequate to correct those mistakes, to ease those situations. Independent police review of the sort that Giuliani has stonewalled would be superfluous here.

The identification with "good cops" that these narratives encourage is further supported by *Brooklyn South*'s relentless effort to divide and conquer the overlapping and conflictual kinds of otherness that characterize the Louima case and, for that matter, everyday life in major U.S. urban centers. The series disentangles the strands of the story of Louima's violation, a complicated story of the anal rape of a Haitian immigrant arrested in front of a Haitian club, which the police claim was also a gay club, by a putatively heterosexual white male police officer engaged to marry an African American woman. *Brooklyn South* then reconstitutes this story into two palatable prime-time narratives. The first is the story of a black man who killed cops and who was thus despised and maybe even assaulted by cops, but who turns out to have died of entirely justifiable gunshot wounds. The second is the story of a white mouthy gay batterer brutalized in what the show, at least, understands to be a nonsexual way by a white police officer who is promptly brought up on charges with the help of his partner and virtually every regular character on the series. In the process, the us vs. them clarity of *Brooklyn South* renders its others simple, clear, and easy to stigmatize, and plays its consensus-forming part in ensuring that all our futures may be marked out in Giuliani Time.

CHAPTER FIVE

Civil Rights, Done and Undone

On July 12, 1999, NAACP president Kweisi Mfume addressed the organization's national convention in New York with a plan to press for changes in the television industry. The occasion for the NAACP's concern was the fact that none of the twenty-six new series on the 1999–2000 fall schedules of ABC, CBS, NBC, and Fox had cast an ethnic minority in a leading role. In Mfume's words, "when the television viewing public sits down to watch the new prime-time shows scheduled for this fall's lineup, they will see a virtual whitewash in programming. . . . This glaring omission is an outrage and a shameful display by network executives who are either clueless, careless or both."[1]

Why was the NAACP, at the end of a century whose problem had indeed turned out to be the color line, and with the devastating effects of that line manifest everywhere one looked, looking at television? What could Mfume have meant when he said that "TV is such an enormous dictator of images, ideas and stereotypes. To ignore that kind of presence in the homes of Americans and the world is to ignore, I think, *the greatest challenge we have*"?[2] What exactly was so outrageous and shameful about this "glaring omission" that it merited the attention of the nation's oldest civil rights organization at a moment when nearly a third of young black men were somehow entangled with the criminal justice system and more than half of black women were raising children below that other decisive line, the poverty line?[3] Why television, and why in 1999?

Three reasons, I think. First, Mfume's move came at a time when the NAACP badly needed to log some well-publicized successes.[4] Plagued by tactical entropy, sexual scandal, and financial malfeasance under Mfume's predecessor, Benjamin Chavis, the NAACP was widely thought to have become irrelevant to contemporary civil rights struggles. According to *Los Angeles Times* reporter Brian Lowry, Mfume "admitted" to ABC's Connie Chung that "he chose this particular battle in part because it was a headline grabbing issue, clearly winnable in the court of public opinion and good publicity for the organization."[5] Clearly, the group's TV "diversity initiative" was part of its efforts to reinvent its own relevance, even as it was paradoxically a return to one of the organization's most reliable past strategies — media activism.[6]

In addition, as the campaign shifted to scrutinize minority representation among the networks' production staffs, writers, and boards of directors, as well as on screen, the effort began to fall more within the NAACP's traditional purview: employment opportunity and economic discrimination.[7] A 1999 survey conducted by the NAACP's Beverly Hills/Hollywood branch and based on the networks' own numbers indicated that of the 839 writers working on prime-time series, only 55 were African American and 83 percent of those were employed on so-called "black shows."[8] So the diversity initiative is legible as a concerted and belated attempt to open up what Mfume has called "the most segregated industry in America" to minorities.[9] Mfume alluded to this aspect of the campaign when asked about the networks' scramble to add minorities to the casts of their new shows: "Our issue is much deeper than that. It's not about adding a black or brown or yellow face. It's about creating equal opportunity for qualified men and women and having products that reflect what this nation really looks like."[10]

Despite Mfume's disclaimer that another "black or brown or yellow face" would answer the NAACP's concerns, his coupling of "equal opportunity" with "products that reflect what this nation really looks like" begins to hint at the campaign's third object: equal opportunity for African Americans *in general* to appear on television. "The airwaves belong to the public," Mfume told the July convention. "African Americans make up 13% of the population; we feel that our presence should be appropriately reflected during prime time."[11] In a December 1999 interview with the *Baltimore Sun*, Mfume underscored this point with the following anecdote: "I remember the time, not too long ago, in communities like the one I grew up in, when you saw somebody black on TV, it was almost your job to run down the street and say 'Hey, come look, there's a Negro on TV.' And everybody quickly got to their televisions and watched. Well, we're almost back there again."[12]

With this story, Mfume deploys a widely told story in African American communities, and imagines a transition from a time, "not too long ago" when a black appearance on television was a neighborhood event, to another time—the present—which is almost as bad as the first, to a future in which black presence is "appropriately reflected."[13] I want to suggest that implicit in this transition is imagined an empowering shift, not only a shift from watching, in Mfume's words, "those shows that make us look invisible" to receiving black figures represented on television as a kind of unremarkable nonevent, but more basically a shift from *watching* television to *being on* television, or at least of having a chance to appear on television commensurate with the African American proportion of the population.[14]

I am suggesting, in other words, a crucial and largely implicit conflation embedded in Mfume's notion of "appropriate reflection," between African Americans being represented on television on one hand, and, on the other, achieving the kinds of empowerment—social, economic, legal—with which the NAACP has been more traditionally concerned. It should not surprise us that Mfume has his own public affairs television show, *The Bottom Line*. For him, as for other African American political and cultural leaders like Jesse Jackson and Henry Louis Gates, the ascendancy to leadership itself corresponds more or less precisely with the ascendancy to televisual celebrity.[15]

But Mfume's imagination of the kinds of cultural efficacy televisibility might have for black people is actually much more complicated than I've suggested so far. For if some African Americans are not visible enough on television, he suggests that others are all too visible. Indeed, Mfume hopes that the "appropriate presence" he envisions will have a specific compensatory effect. In his words,

> If you're able to see people of different colors, different backgrounds and different roles repetitively on this medium we call television, it counteracts and counterbalances what you see on the small segment we call the news. The news gives you the worst of the worst, people in handcuffs or shackles, or photos of criminals who are wanted by the police.
>
> A lot of people look at that small part, the news, and make decisions about a whole group.
>
> We believe that the larger part of television, if it is balanced, and if it is sending the right message, it benefits all Americans. It enables them to look at the small picture, the news, and say there are bad people out there who are black, white and members of every race and group, but there is more, a larger picture, too. And that helps to create a more tolerant society.[16]

Here we find that the problem isn't, in fact, that "we're almost back" to the time when a black presence on television was a neighborhood event. It's rather that the news—by which here Mfume clearly means the local news—reproduces all too commonly *certain kinds* of black performance, among them the mug shot or the so-called "perp walk." Mfume is right about this; since he watches the same local news that I do, in Baltimore, I can attest that the routines of local news there (and presumably in other largely black cities) overwhelmingly collate blackness with criminality, addiction, and the underclass. So it turns out that the problem with American television in 1999 for Mfume's NAACP is that it underrepresents "difference," resolving the diversity within African American communities into the endless repetition of the perp walk. Since by "difference" Mfume seems to mean here social markers like class, education, and occupation, the "larger picture" he advocates would be "balanced," would send "the right message," by representing more middle-class blacks and fewer "criminal" ones.

Indeed, we might describe the NAACP's television problem as a putative imbalance in the medium's deployment of two of its most cherished racial tropes. On one hand, Herman Gray has written about what he calls "the civil rights subject," the successful, well-educated, articulate middle-class black who is an exemplary consumer and citizen (think *The Cosby Show*'s Cliff Huxtable, sweaters blazing) and even a highly placed guardian of law and order (think *Homicide*'s Giardello, *NYPD Blue*'s Fancy, *Law and Order*'s Van Buren).[17] Opposed to the civil rights subject, often within the same texts, is the second trope, which I have come to think of as "the subject of civil rights undone" — undone in the sense of unfinished, dismantled, or rejected. The subject of civil rights undone comprises representations of blacks as crack addicts, homeless people, teenage mothers, gang-bangers, drug dealers, and children threatened by "random" ghetto violence.

But Mfume's analysis of the relation between the news and the rest of the television flow is missing something crucial here: the way in which the civil rights subject and the subject of civil rights undone each depend utterly on the tropological production of the other, just as Martin's mediated image has come to depend on that of Malcolm, and vice versa.[18] Drawing upon and revising earlier organizing dichotomies, like the house slave/field slave or Washington/Dubois binaries, television conjured the civil rights subject and the subject of civil rights undone, and made Martin and Malcolm exemplars of them at about the same time, establishing their oppositional relation almost immediately. In network documentaries like ABC's 1961 *Bell and Howell Close-Up* "Walk in My Shoes," and *CBS Reports*' 1963 "The Harlem Temper," for example, the Nation of Islam, embodied in particular by Malcolm X, is offered up as the terrifying specter of what will emerge in places like Harlem if the "reasonable" demands of nonviolent civil rights demonstrators, embodied in particular by King, aren't met.[19] American culture has used them as a tag team ever since. Thus Mfume's dream of "balanced" television misunderstands that, often as not, these figures reinforce rather than counteract each other.

More important, though, it misunderstands the extent of the ideological and political damage that has been done to black people by the civil rights subject, which, as Gray argues, has a hyper-visibility all its own. Television, he writes, "is constantly engaged in a kind of recuperative work, a kind of retrospective production of raced and gendered subjects who fit the requirements of contemporary circumstance" particularly via "representations of those black, largely middle-class benefactors who gained the most *visibility* as well as material and status rewards from the struggles and opportunities generated by the civil rights movement. This cultural figure embodies complex codes of behavior and propriety that make it an exemplar of citizenship and responsibility — success, mobility, hard work, sacrifice, individualism."[20] This figure, Gray notes, is indispensable for the racial projects of post-Reagan America, helping to "construct the mythic terms through which many Americans can believe that our nation has now transcended racism."[21]

Thus far, I've sought to demonstrate that two under-theorized assumptions structure the NAACP's understanding of African American televisual representation and its consequent actions in relation to the contemporary television industry. The first is that the representation of African Americans on television in numbers commensurate with our numbers in the population would itself be empowering for African Americans, above and beyond the material benefits to be reaped by individuals through televisual publicity. The second is that the cause of black people might be advanced by greater "balance" between the representation of the subject of civil rights undone and the civil rights subject. The former argues for the political force of raw numbers, while the latter insists that raw numbers themselves are insufficient, because only certain kinds of representations will support the cause of black empowerment.

Though these assumptions about the relation between television and African American advancement are wrong in the ways I've been suggesting, they are nonetheless both widespread. In imagining that new forms of economic, cultural, and political power might await those who cross the line from watching to being watched, Mfume reproduces a persistent theme in postwar African American culture, one that certainly has to do with the deep connection, in African American cultural memory, of television to the civil rights movement, of an electronic medium to a moment of exploding opportunity. And the notion that only representations of exemplary persons will serve the race is one that long predates television.

In the rest of this chapter, I hope to complicate these assumptions about the meanings of contemporary African American representation by reading several films that imagine television as playing a central role in constituting black subjectivity, publicity, and political effectivity: Spike Lee's 1992 *Malcolm X*, Russell Mulcahy's 1991 *Ricochet*, and the Hughes Brothers' 1993 *Menace II Society*. All share a sense of both the vicissitudes of visual mediation and the inextricability of the civil rights subject from the subject of civil rights undone. All share the knowledge of how quickly ordinary publicity, for the subject of civil rights, can turn into surveillance. And all share a certain ironic (and perhaps even hostile) distance from television; the cultural roles and social functions of the apparatus constitute for each an object of critical inquiry. I turn to these films in the hopes that the understandings of television they offer may help sharpen our expectations of television's role within African American struggles.

MALCOLM X ON TV

Spike Lee's *Malcolm X* understands that the civil rights subject and the subject of civil rights undone are crucially televisual productions. Indeed, in the two sequences I will discuss, the film dramatizes the making and deployment of these tropes on and by television, using representatives from the SCLC and the NAACP on one hand, and from the Nation of Islam on the other, as their most visible exemplars. Since Lee's project in general valorizes Malcolm's nationalist politics over King's nonviolence — Lee has been quoted as saying "the whole nonviolent, turn-the-other-cheek business just isn't getting anywhere in black America" — the film, not surprisingly, reverses the hegemonic hierarchical ordering of these figures to privilege the subject of civil rights undone.[22] Lee's *Malcolm* relates to television both as a critical counterspectator to the kind of network civil rights discourse I've described in chapter 1, and as a counterperformer insisting that television is a stage on which race may be contested.

In the first sequence, Lee cross-cuts among three scenes: Malcolm (Denzel Washington) giving a speech to a large crowd, with Elijah Muhammad (Al Freeman, Jr.) seated on the podium behind him; Malcolm's wife, Betty (Angela Bassett), at home with their first daughter; and Malcolm in a hotel room watching television. Betty is here as a sign of the domestic and to provide plot exposition — to tell us in voice-over that their daughter has been born, and that Malcolm is touring the country dedicating new temples. She is also here to demonstrate the irrelevance of women to the televisual transactions of image-making and consumption that preoccupy Malcolm in the other two scenes.[23]

Malcolm's speech, the longest and most forceful depicted in the film, is organized around refuting two related complaints often lodged against the Nation of Islam: that Elijah Muhammad's teaching is "hate teaching" and that the Nation advocates "black supremacy."[24] The occasion allows him to reiterate the Nation's principles of economic self-determination and self-defense in the face of white violence. It is in the exposition of the latter point that Malcolm takes on the civil rights movement:

> The black people in this country have been the victims of violence at the hands of the American white man for four hundred years. Four hundred

years. *Four hundred years.* And we thought, by following those ignorant Negro preachers, that it was godlike to turn the other cheek to the brute that
was brutalizing us. One hundred years ago, they used to put on white sheets
and sick bloodhounds on us. Nowadays they've traded in the sheets—well,
some of them have traded in the sheets—for police uniforms, they've traded
in the bloodhounds for police dogs. And just like that old Uncle Tom back
during slavery time, they try to . . . stop you and I from resisting the Ku Klux
Klan, from resisting the dogs by teaching us to love our enemies and pray for
those who use us spitefully. You've got those chicken pecking Uncle Tom so-
called Negro leaders today . . . that are telling us we ought to pray for our
enemy, we ought to love our enemy, we ought to integrate with an enemy
who bombs us, who kills and shoots us, who lynches us, who rapes our
women and children. No, no, no. That's not intelligent.

The speech is intercut with a set of similar shot/reverse shots: Malcolm,
sitting on a bed in a generic sixties hotel room, and black-and-white
television news footage of the southern civil rights movement, first
clearly framed by the borders of a diegetic television screen, then expanding to fill the entire film frame (fig. 5.1). As the speech continues in
voice-over, Malcolm watches scenes of fire hoses and police dogs wielded
against black demonstrators in Birmingham, of police beating and arresting protestors in a variety of locations, of participants in the Nashville sit-ins beaten and abused, of churches and houses firebombed, of
Klan rallies.

Rather than encouraging us to see these images of racial brutality and
black nonviolence as evidence of African American nobility and courage
(as, for example, something like *Eyes on the Prize* tends to), this painstakingly edited sequence teaches us to see it through Malcolm's eyes,
rendering the footage a series of illustrations of his criticisms of the
southern movement.[25] Images of Martin Luther King and Roy Wilkins
(including one of Wilkins grinning like a fool) are carefully timed to
coincide with phrases like "ignorant Negro preachers" and "chicken-
pecking Uncle Tom so-called Negro leaders." And the repetitive images
of white police beating black protesters not only emphasizes the violence of "the American white man," but also succeeds in making the
practices of nonviolent blacks look like a pathological passivity. The
sequence, in other words, simultaneously demonstrates how Malcolm
might have watched such footage and teaches the film's spectators to
engage in a similar kind of counterspectatorship.

Television in this sequence *means* the southern civil rights movement,
but *Malcolm X* is careful not to fall into an easy condemnation of television for its association with integrationists. In the sequence immediately following the one I've described, *Malcolm X* looks at the appa-

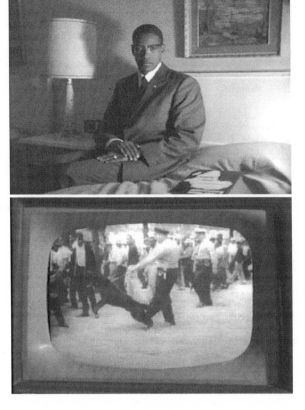

FIGURE 5.1.
Malcolm watches
television.

ratus from the inside out when Malcolm himself appears on TV. The first shot (fig. 5.2 top) of the sequence focuses on television monitors in a studio control room, then pans (fig. 5.2 middle) to a shot of Malcolm on the set of the fictitious public affairs program *Our World Today* (fig. 5.2 bottom), as the host (Craig Wasson) introduces the episode's topic "Black Muslims: Hate-Mongers." The title of the program obviously cites Mike Wallace and Louis Lomax's 1959 television documentary on the Nation, *The Hate that Hate Produced*, another clue to the film's awareness of television's necessary role in producing both Malcolm as a public figure and the larger trope he has come to epitomize.

But *Malcolm X* insists that Malcolm, too, is at least co-producing this TV show. On *Our World Today* Malcolm squares off against another Uncle Tom, or, as Malcolm has it, "house Negro," Dr. Payson (Graham Brown), showcasing the ferocity of his intelligence and the dexterity of his rhetoric.[26] The film here underscores the importance of Malcolm's performance by insisting vigorously on his *being watched*. Indeed, it is

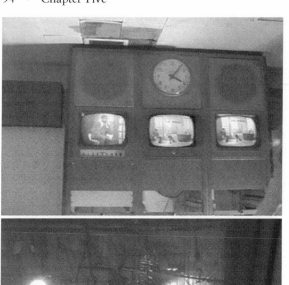

FIGURE 5.2.
Malcolm on TV.

FIGURE 5.3.
Baines and
Muhammad
watch
Malcolm.

willing to break certain rules of continuity editing to do so: twice the film cuts from a two-shot of Malcolm and Payson to a shot of the studio audience from between their heads, a violation of the "180° rule." And if that wasn't enough, Lee cross-cuts throughout the sequence between the television studio and Elijah Muhammad and Baines (Albert Hall) watching Malcolm on television (fig. 5.3). As Baines and Muhammad watch, Baines broaches for the first time the possibility that Malcolm may be becoming too powerful, thus establishing definitively, for *Malcolm X*, the link between being powerful and being televised.

Through its juxtaposition of Baines's treachery with Malcolm's telegenicity, and through the introduction, later in the film, of what we

FIGURE 5.4. CIA-cam on Malcolm at Mecca.

might call the "CIA-cam" — the 8mm color films of Malcolm shot by the two white men who follow him to Mecca and interspliced with *Malcolm X*'s "proper" images — the film begins to explore the relationship, for black subjects, between being on television and being surveilled by image-making technology (fig. 5.4). Another Denzel Washington film, *Ricochet*, begins to explore this question more fully.

THE NICK STYLES SHOW

Ricochet is the story of an up-and-coming black public official, Nick Styles (Washington), who at the beginning of the film is working as an LAPD officer and attending law school at night. One night, on patrol at a street fair with his partner, Larry (Kevin Pollak), Styles foils a crime in progress, perpetuated by up-and-coming white criminal Earl Talbot Blake (John Lithgow). Styles and Blake face off; Blake, armed with an enormous shotgun, is also holding a woman hostage. Styles, to persuade Blake that he is unarmed, not only puts down his gun, but actually strips to his briefs, all the while urging Blake to "let the girl go," and offering himself as an alternate hostage. Blake does release the woman, but tries to attack Styles with a knife just as Styles pulls a small pistol from the back of his briefs and shoots Blake in the kneecap, disabling him sufficiently that he can be apprehended.

As its opening suggests, *Ricochet* will go on to pursue with relish the by-now-naturalized conventions of the Hollywood paranoid gothic, with all its attendant queering effects.[27] Not surprisingly, women serve in this film strictly as indicators of male status or as objects of exchange between men. Indeed, women are so irrelevant to *Ricochet* that we don't learn Styles's wife's name until the closing credits! The film is too busy literalizing the televisual production of Styles as a civil rights subject — a process it understands as indicatively male — to offer such a minor detail. Here's how the process works.

With the help of an amateur video shot by a bystander at his face-off with Blake (fig. 5.5), Styles becomes a TV celebrity and is immediately promoted to detective. When he finishes law school, right after serving as the star of a special episode of *Busted!* (a rip-off of *Cops*; fig. 5.6), he immediately becomes L.A.'s most visible assistant district attorney. As if performing perfectly a script entitled "Black Success Story: Working Within the System" — a script clearly written, not by Styles, but by the various bosses and handlers who appear in the wake of Blake's arrest like roaches in a darkened kitchen — he marries the aforementioned unnamed woman he met in the film's first scene, has two perfect children, and goes to live in a big house in an exclusive part of town. Thus he

FIGURE 5.5. Styles's first encounter with Blake caught on tape.

FIGURE 5.6. Styles stars in an episode of *Busted*.

leaves behind his old 'hood, where his father (John Amos) is a preacher, and his best friend from childhood, Odessa (Ice-T), is the head of a crack ring.[28] But Styles tries to help those whom he leaves behind by spearheading a campaign for a youth center at the base of the Watts Towers, planning to raise money for the project with a telethon (fig. 5.7).

Blake, meanwhile, is in prison, having come to understand, while watching Styles on television, that revenge against Styles can restore to his life the purpose that his incarceration has taken from him. Though his hatred of Styles is depicted by the film as purely "personal" (i.e., not racially motivated), he is not above enlisting the help of a group of inmates calling themselves the Aryan Brotherhood to engineer his escape. He breaks out of prison, carefully making it look as though he's been killed in the attempt, and begins an intricate reign of terror against Styles that is designed to "deconstruct," to borrow the film's own term, Styles's public persona. Adroitly manipulating television's appetite for

FIGURE 5.7. Styles hosts a telethon to raise money for a youth center.

stories of black male malfeasance—its appetite, in other words, for moments in which the civil rights subject and the subject of civil rights undone seem to collapse into one another—Blake takes over from the bosses and handlers the role of head scriptwriter for Styles's life, inserting Styles into a narrative of racially coded corruption and disgrace that the bewildered Styles can't help but perform. He implicates Styles in pedophilia and theft, injects him with drugs, videotapes him having sex with a white prostitute, and dumps him on the steps of City Hall, where he is discovered among a motley collection of homeless people. Finally, Blake kills Styles's ex-partner, Larry, and tosses the gun to Styles, thus insuring that Styles will be charged with Larry's death and Blake will be treated to the spectacle of his televised arrest.

At this point, Styles gets serious. After admonishing his children not to watch him on TV when he's with them "in real life," and finally destroying the family TV by knocking it off its stand, he determines to become at last the writer, producer, and director of his own life. With the help of Odessa and Odessa's entire crack ring, he stages a show for the television news cameras, thus luring Blake out of hiding and enticing him to their final rendezvous at the Watts Towers: he stands on top of Odessa's building, announces the beginning of "The Nick Styles Show," paints himself with clown makeup, and stages his own death in a parody of Blake's fake demise (fig. 5.8). When the "Show" changes locations and moves to the Towers, Odessa's posse carefully allows TV news crews access to the area so that they can witness the fight to the death, which ends with Blake impaled on a spike(!), his corpse definitive proof that Blake—thought dead after the prison break—has in fact recently been alive to orchestrate his campaign against Styles. The film ends as Styles takes final control over the televisual apparatus by turning off a camera in the midst of a live broadcast (fig. 5.9).

As I hope this summary has already begun to suggest, *Ricochet* is

FIGURE 5.8. "The Nick Styles Show."

fairly confused (or pretends, cynically, to be confused) about whether race is, in fact, a determining force in the sociality it depicts. On one hand, it undoes two of the more powerful contemporary media discourses which can still imagine that anything is "racially motivated": representations of law enforcement's overzealous policing of both criminalized black bodies and African American public officials. By carefully placing an amateur video maker at the scene of Styles's first encounter with Blake, the film restages the attack on Rodney King by recasting King as a deranged white killer and depicting the cops in a harmonious biracial partnership in which they display admirably restrained escalation of force. And by insisting that Blake is out to get Styles because Blake is a homicidal maniac, not because Styles is black, the film reinscribes our national penchant for undermining black politicians in ways that obscure racial motivations.

On the other hand, though, *Ricochet* seems ultimately to argue for the utter necessity of racially based, cross-class alliances. After all, as the text on the back of the video version insists, "To defeat Blake, Nick

FIGURE 5.9. Styles turns off the television.

must return to the streets, calling on his old friend Odessa. Together they set a trap that pits Nick against the killer in a terrifying confrontation that will leave one man victorious — and only one man left alive." In other words, the film suggests in its closing moments, as Styles and Odessa make plans to play basketball together the following Saturday, that one of the life lessons Nick Styles has learned from being stalked by Earl Talbot Blake is that old friends should come before an over-literal adherence to the law. We leave the film assured that the mere fact that Odessa is a crack dealer and Styles is an assistant district attorney will no longer come between them.

Ricochet's desire for this happy alliance between the civil rights subject and the subject of civil rights undone leads the film into some important narrative predicaments. We first meet Odessa in the opening scene, in which he, his friend R.C., Styles, and Larry are playing basketball. Amid the trash-talking and ribbing of Larry for playing like a white boy, Odessa and Styles clearly exhibit a longstanding masculine intimacy, marked particularly by Odessa's incessant deployment of Styles's childhood nickname: P.K., for "preacher's kid." At the end of the scene, though, Styles and Odessa part uncomfortably and, it seems, permanently. Noticing that Odessa is driving a new, expensive, and hotwired car, Styles, about to get into his police cruiser, says ruefully, "I think our playing days are over." With this, Odessa disappears from the film until Styles goes to see him in the crack house to warn him away from the children's center: "You don't sell no dope there, you don't recruit, you don't bang, none of that." When Odessa refuses, asking, "and why the fuck should I do that?" Styles replies, in heavily coded "street" cadences that my transcription can only suggest:

> For your mother . . . nigger, the one died of a broken heart praying with my father every night over your black ass. The one that buried your little brother without his head 'cause they couldn't find it. . . . Look, Odessa, I know you ain't gonna change, but don't cheat these kids out of their future, man. . . . Do the right thing, my brother.

When Odessa remains unmoved by the eloquence of his old friend, Styles pulls out a grenade, saying that he's not afraid to die for what *he* believes in, and challenging Odessa and his crew to do the same. Cut to an exterior shot, in which Styles rejoins his former partner, Larry, and reveals the grenade to be a mere cigarette lighter.

At this point, it seems important to point out that *Ricochet*'s screenplay, which was written by Steven DeSouza (*48 Hrs.*, *Die Hard*, *Die Harder*) is as tightly put-together as any script of its genre, and it's put together considerably more tightly than most. That is to say, this film has a more than adequately developed sense of narrative causality. With this in mind, the elisions in this scene, and in the narrative developments that follow it, are striking. We never learn how, or even whether, Styles and Odessa resolve their differences, or how Styles gets out of the building. This gap is rendered even more noticeable by the fact that this scene is the last we see of Odessa until Styles turns to him for help in his fight against Blake. For some reason that the film only half-heartedly tries to explain, Odessa is not only willing to help his old friend, but is willing to blow up his headquarters, destroy his drug-processing lab, and risk his own life in the process. Now, it seems far from coincidental to me that this scene, in addition to being the point at which the narrative makes the least sense, is also the moment in which we see the heretofore ebonically impaired Styles performing, via drastically altered diction, his identity as Odessa's former homeboy. Indeed, it may be the collision of Styles's sudden verbal "blackness" with his chosen role as The Law that produces the incoherence of this scene and of Styles and Odessa's subsequent encounter. And, crucially, this conflict is amplified and reproduced by the crash of Styles's self-righteousness against o.g. Odessa's economic pragmatism.

Another way to describe what happens in this scene is to view the intersection of the civil rights subject with the subject of civil rights undone as putting a kind of intolerable pressure on this film. *Ricochet* can endlessly devour and regurgitate the conflict between Blake and Styles, precisely because it is putatively "random" with respect to race and class. But because the contests elaborated here—between Styles's past and present class positions, and between Odessa and Styles—are properly social conflicts that the film hopes both to exploit and ignore, they can only send the narrative into disarray. And it is because *Ricochet* understands that both these subjects are crucially made and unmade by televisual tropes—admiring news coverage for black men like Styles, and the harsh lighting and digitized faces of *Busted!* for black men like Odessa—that the film turns its focus to TV (which, not coincidentally, is prominent in the crack house mise-en-scène) as a way of evading this problem. Side-stepping the question of class in favor of what it posits as a representational problem, in other words, the film foregrounds the battle between Blake and Styles over Styles's depiction on television. At this point Odessa has disappeared again, only to reemerge at precisely the moment in which Styles aggressively retakes control over his mediated image. *Ricochet* thus seems to suggest that a black counterpublicity made manifest through televisual authorship and performance might provide an opening for intraracial class alliance. On the other hand, it also seems to suggest that such counterpublicity is likely, or even possible, only under the pressure of bizarre circumstances.

VIDEO SURVEILLANCE AND COUNTERSPECTATORSHIP

I have considered the centrality of television—as an object, an apparatus, and a discourse—to our collective understandings of contemporary black social, cultural, and political life. I have discussed TV's production of two crucial tropes of blackness: the civil rights subject and the subject of civil rights undone. And I have argued more specifically that *Ricochet* averts its gaze from the material intractability of intraracial class relations to gape instead at a struggle for control over televisual encoding and dissemination. It would not be an overstatement to say that *Ricochet*'s obsession with Nick Styles's performances renders the film completely uninterested in questions of reception: it assumes that everyone who is not a sociopath or an hysteric will read Styles's televisual image within a strictly dominant paradigm, a paradigm in which Styles is a hero before Blake's escape and a deviant, drug-addicted, adulterous cop-killer after.[29] Now I want to turn briefly to another recent film that shares *Ricochet*'s fascination with television, but which figures that fascination in terms of spectatorship rather than performance.

Menace II Society may be less oversaturated with television than *Ricochet*, but television and video play a crucial role in its narrative as well. The opening scene insists that Caine and O-Dog dwell in a Los Angeles in which "racial and class polarization," in Grant Farred's words, "wears the highly public face of sophisticated security and surveillance systems."[30] And not so sophisticated ones. As Caine and O-Dog move through an urban, Asian-owned liquor store, anticipating a party that night which will be abundantly populated with "bitches," they are observed so closely and obviously by its owners that they confront them openly about their assumptions that they will steal something. Street savvy as they are, Caine and O-Dog know that they are always being watched, and they understand thoroughly the visual and narrative tropes that overdetermine their appearances as subjects of civil rights undone. The film makes this fact even more pointed when O-Dog, after shooting one of the owners for dissing his mother, compels the other owner to give him the surveillance tape before he shoots and kills her as well.

Paula Massood has argued that while the surveillance video comprises "an innovative means of conveying action," it is ultimately a "red herring" that "never connects directly to the film's later events."[31] But while the video may not play a central role in the film's plot, its ideological function is crucial, as it insists that, unlike Styles, or even Malcolm, Caine and O-Dog cannot contest the fundamental stories told about them by the visual technologies that surround them. Their resistance — as subjects of civil rights undone — can only take the form of reframing those stories within an alternative set of reception practices. This explains why O-Dog risks playing the tape over and over again for his friends at parties, despite Caine's objections (fig. 5.10).

Menace is careful to connect the contemporary, video-based strategies of surveillance Caine and O-Dog encounter daily to their strong precursors in television news coverage of Watts. The first few minutes of the film make this connection explicit. After Caine and O-Dog leave the convenience store, the camera holds for several seconds on the door through which they've just exited. In voice-over, Caine observes, "Went in to get a beer, came out an accessory to murder and armed robbery. It was funny like that in the hood sometimes. You never knew what was going to happen, or when. After that," here the screen fades to black, "I knew it was gonna be a long summer." Fade into the first title card, "New Line Cinema presents," as Walter Cronkite's voice becomes audible on the soundtrack:

Nearly one thousand persons rioted in the Watts District last night. They attacked police with rock, bricks and bottles before some one hundred . . .

FIGURE 5.10.
O-Dog and friends
watch the robbery
video.

On "one hundred," the voice of another newscaster joins Cronkite's
and continues over the "A New Line Production" title card:

> one hundred officers sealed off the four block area in the vicinity of 116th
> Street and Avalon Boulevard. Four persons were arrested . . .

Here "A Hughes Brothers Film" as the voice continues and is joined again by Cronkite:

A number of others, including one policeman, were injured in the melee.

Over the final title, "Menace II Society," Cronkite's voice continues alone:

The riot was touched off when three drunk drivers . . .

Then a twenty-shot sequence of television news footage of the riots, mostly pixillated, under a soundtrack combining police radio calls, news commentary, diegetic sound, sirens, gunshots, and the chant "Burn, Baby, Burn." Over the final shot of the sequence, of a black boy walking around a burned-out building, Caine's voice again: "When the riots stopped, the drugs started."

Structurally linked to the opening of the film by the fact that their soundtracks begin before we see their accompanying images, and by the fact that Caine's voice-overs serve as sound bridges to what follows, this sequence, with its multiplying hegemonic voices and its relentless repetition of images of black bodies beaten by whites, reminds us of the historical connection among the ethnographic regard brought to bear on the inner city by TV news cameras, the not-so-veiled threats to blacks contained within their graphic depictions of the reassertion of law and order, and the panoptic promise of postmodern urban policing. But if these sequences implicitly couple police cross-hairs with the video frame, the distantiation effect produced by the pixillation of the televisual image in the Watts section suggests that while the resistant spectatorship of O-Dog many serve only to dig him and Caine deeper into the morass of the 'hood, the resistant spectatorship of the Hughes Brothers may prove more politically efficacious. Indeed, the acuity of Allen and Albert Hughes's reading of television and video connects *Menace* to the ongoing project of African American media critique in a way that avoids the metaphysical dead end of the good images/bad images debate.

But it also suggests, perhaps in spite of itself, the limitations of that project for African American subjects in general. It is crucial, I think, that Caine and O-Dog talk of "bitches" in the opening sequence, and that black women remain outside the frame of that determining scene of action. Indeed, insofar as *Menace* understands the video frame to indicate the field of African American subjection and the resistant reception of that frame to comprise a practice which might contest that subjection, the film's inability to imagine black women anywhere in the encoding/decoding loop undermines whatever progressive possibilities for spectatorship the film offers. For *Menace*, as for American television itself, African American women tend to remain in the space-off of video representation.

It is worth recalling, in this regard, Lyndon Johnson's response to seeing Fannie Lou Hamer's televised testimony at the 1964 Democratic convention in Atlantic City. Hamer was representing the Mississippi Freedom Democratic Party, asking the credentials committee that the MFDP be seated instead of the segregated delegation sent by Mississippi's democratic party. Johnson, knowing that he would lose the south if the Mississippi "regulars" weren't seated, displaced her image and words with his own, preempting convention coverage with an impromptu speech from the White House.[32]

I cite this story not to suggest an equivalence between Johnson and the Hughes Brothers, but rather to underscore the historically intractable closure of television to the representation of African American women and our political critique. This intractability imposes yet another limit on the efficacy of interventions on behalf of black political advancement that take television as their object. If television is ambivalent about the politicized black male subjects it generates and cannibalizes, it generally exiles black women from its frame altogether.

Notes

ABBREVIATIONS USED IN NOTES

Archives

LOC	Motion Picture, Broadcasting and Recorded Sound Division, Library of Congress, Washington
MBC	Museum of Broadcast Communications, Chicago
KLA	King Library and Archives, Martin Luther King, Jr., Center for Nonviolent Social Change, Atlanta
MTR	Museum of Television and Radio, New York and Los Angeles
UCLA	UCLA Film and Television Archive, Los Angeles

Manuscript Collections at King Library and Archives

CORE	The papers of the Congress of Racial Equality
MLK	The papers of Martin Luther King, Jr.
SCLC	Southern Christian Leadership Conference Records
Shuttlesworth	The papers of Rev. Fred W. Shuttlesworth
SNCC	Student Nonviolent Coordinating Committee Records

INTRODUCTION

1. Jannette L. Dates and William Barlow, eds., *Split Image: African Americans in the Mass Media* (Washington, D.C.: Howard University Press, 1990). Other scholarly accounts that lean heavily on the stereotype for their conceptual apparatus are J. Fred MacDonald, *Blacks and White TV: African Americans in Television since 1948*, 2nd ed. (Chicago: Nelson Hall, 1992) and Patricia A. Turner, *Ceramic Uncles and Celluloid Mammies: Black Images and Their Influences on Culture* (New York: Anchor, 1994). Donald Bogle's work on American film has also been widely influential among television scholars. See especially the taxonomy of stereotypes he elaborates in *Toms, Coons, Mulattoes, Mammies, and Bucks: An Interpretive History of Blacks in American Film*, new rev. ed. (New York: Continuum, 1991). Some recent work that approaches the question of African American television representation from other angles includes Herman Gray, *Watching Race: Television and the Struggle for "Blackness"* (Minneapolis: University of Minnesota Press, 1995); Phillip Brian Harper, "Extra-Special Effects: Televisual Representation and the Claims of the 'Black Experience,'" in *Living Color: Race and Television in the United States*, ed. Sasha Torres (Durham: Duke University Press, 1998), 62–81; and Noliwe Rooks, "By Any Other Name: *Sweet Justice*, Cicely Tyson, and Contemporary Racial Politics," *Camera Obscura*, no. 36 (1995): 49–66.

2. Dates and Barlow, *Split Image*, 3.

3. On *Amos 'n' Andy*, see Melvin Patrick Ely, *The Adventures of Amos 'n'*

Andy: A Social History of an American Phenomenon (New York: Free Press, 1991) and Thomas Cripps, "*Amos 'n' Andy* and the Debate over American Racial Integration," in *American History/American Television: Interpreting the Video Past*, ed. John E. O'Connor (New York: Ungar, 1983), 33–54. I discuss a more recent NAACP action with respect to television in the conclusion

4. My point here is indebted to Eve Kosofsky Sedgwick, particularly to her "The Beast in the Closet: James and the Writing of Homosexual Panic," in *Epistemology of the Closet* (Berkeley: University of California Press, 1990).

5. Henry Louis Gates, Jr., *Colored People: A Memoir* (New York: Knopf, 1994), 22, original emphasis.

6. bell hooks, *Yearning: Race, Gender and Cultural Politics* (Boston: South End, 1990).

7. On "flow," see Raymond Williams, *Television: Technology and Cultural Form* (New York: Schocken, 1975). On viewer's television archives, see Robert H. Deming, "*Kate and Allie*: 'New Women' and the Audience's Television Archives," in *Private Screenings*, ed. Lynn Spigel and Denise Mann (Minneapolis: Minnesota, 1992), 203–16.

8. Richard Dyer, *White* (New York: Routledge, 1997).

9. My allusion to deferential depictions was inspired by Sharon Willis's discussion of "the ubiquitous African American judge[s] or police chief[s]" who populate contemporary film and television and "exhibit racial difference, but sideline it so that they also help to hedge ideological bets." See her *High Contrast: Race and Gender in Contemporary Hollywood Film* (Durham: Duke University Press, 1997), 5.

10. On the ethnographic tendencies of documentary featuring blacks, see Herman Gray, "Television, Black Americans, and the American Dream," *Critical Studies in Mass Communication* 6 (1989): 376–86 and Michael Curtin, *Redeeming the Wasteland: Television Documentary and Cold War Politics* (New Brunswick: Rutgers University Press, 1995).

11. For vibrant examples of the ways in which television's coverage of mass racial politics condenses and condescends, see transcripts of *Meet the Press* for 25 August 1963, SCLC, KLA, box 27, folder 16; 28 March 1965, SCLC, KLA, box 4, folder 42; and 21 August 1966, SNCC, KLA, box 5, folder "Meet the Press."

12. 5 December 1967 letter from Peggy Whedon to Martin Luther King, Jr., MLK, KLA, box 2, folder 16. The correspondence I was able to locate in the MLK papers between King's office and *Issues and Answers* runs from 1965, when King apparently missed a scheduled appearance due to events in Selma, to Whedon's last letter to McDonald on 13 March 1968. The letters are frequently marked by Whedon's frustration at King's apparent tendency to value appearances on the more prestigious *Face the Nation* over those on her show. See especially Whedon's letters in MLK, KLA, box 2, folder 16 and box 39, folder 41.

13. 11 January 1968 letter from Dora McDonald to Peggy Whedon, MLK, KLA, box 2, folder 16.

14. 22 January 1968 letter from Peggy Whedon to Dora McDonald, MLK, KLA, box 2, folder 16.

15. 30 January 1968 letter from Dora McDonald to Peggy Whedon, MLK, KLA, box 2, folder 16.

16. 13 February 1968 letter from Peggy Whedon to Dora McDonald, MLK, KLA, box 3, folder 16.

17. On catastrophe coverage, see Mary Ann Doane, "Information, Crisis, Catastrophe," in *Logics of Television*, ed. Patricia Mellencamp (Bloomington: Indiana University Press, 1990), 222–39. On media events, see Daniel Dayan and Elihu Katz, *Media Events: The Live Broadcasting of History* (Cambridge: Harvard University Press, 1992).

18. In this important regard, MacDonald's *Blacks and White TV* differs from Dates and Barlow's *Split Image*, in that it pays considerable attention to the tensions between entertainment and informational programming during the medium's early period. Though it doesn't put as much pressure on these tensions as I might like, it does provide a wealth of information on where one might look to begin reading these contradictions.

19. For example, see Glen Feldman, *Politics, Society, and the Klan in Alabama, 1915–1949* (Tuscaloosa: University of Alabama Press, 1999); Richard K. Tucker, *The Dragon and the Cross: The Rise and Fall of the Ku Klux Klan in Middle America* (Hamden, Conn.: Archon, 1991); Kathleen M. Blee, *Women of the Klan: Racism and Gender in the 1920s* (Berkeley: University of California Press, 1991); and Wyn Craig Wade, *The Fiery Cross: The Ku Klux Klan in America* (New York: Simon & Schuster, 1987).

20. Michael Omi and Howard Winant, *Racial Formation in the United States: From the 1960s to the 1990s*, 2nd ed. (New York: Routledge, 1994), 117.

21. Herman Gray, *Watching Race: Television and the Struggle for "Blackness"* (Minneapolis: University of Minnesota Press, 1995), 18.

22. See David Farber, "The Silent Majority and Talk about Revolution," in *The Sixties: From Memory to History*, ed. David Farber (Chapel Hill: University of North Carolina Press, 1994), 291–316.

23. Kimberlé Crenshaw, "Race, Reform, and Retrenchment: Transformation and Legitimation in Antidiscrimination Law," in *Critical Race Theory: The Key Writings That Formed the Movement*, ed. Kimberlé Crenshaw, Neil Gotanda, Gary Peller, and Kendall Thomas (New York: New Press, 1995), 103–104.

24. Derrick Bell offers a brief history of this strategy, first developed in 1938. See his "Serving Two Masters: Integration Ideals and Client Interests in School Desegregation Litigation," in *Critical Race Theory*, 6–7.

25. Crenshaw, "Race, Reform, and Retrenchment," 105. In the same volume, *Critical Race Theory*, see also Alan David Freeman, "Legitimizing Racial Discrimination through Antidiscrimination Law: A Critical Review of Supreme Court Doctrine," 9–46 and Gary Peller, "Race-Consciousness," 127–58.

26. Gray, *Watching Race*, 23.

27. Ibid., 17–18.

28. For more on this, see chapter 1.

29. Gray, *Watching Race*, 17.

30. Ibid., 34.

31. One of the best sources on race and television news in the 1980s is Jim-

mie L. Reeves and Richard Campbell, *Cracked Coverage: Television News, the Anti-Cocaine Crusade, and the Reagan Legacy* (Durham: Duke University Press, 1994).

32. Eighties television news and '90s fictional law and order programming are linked, I believe, by a transitional genre invented at the intersection of the two decades: reality television. For if TV news in the '80s taught us not to identify with blackness by equating it with criminality, violence, addiction, and irresponsibility, *Cops* and *America's Most Wanted* taught us to identify with law enforcement, whose viewpoint completely organizes the series' narratives and visual style. In *Cops*, the police provide the voice-over or direct-address narration that maps the urban landscapes through which we travel in police cruisers. And these landscapes are made visible to us by a camera situated just behind the heads of the officers in the patrol cars. By figuratively inviting us to see the world through the eyes of the police, the show neatly sutures us into the cops' preexisting relation (varying from contempt to condescension) with the Others of these cityscapes. This kind of spectatorship proved excellent practice, it turned out, for watching programs about law and policing in the 1990s. For more on this, see chapter 4.

33. Harper, "Extra-Special Effects," 70–72.

34. Jane Feuer, "The Concept of Live Television: Ontology as Ideology," *Regarding Television—Critical Approaches: An Anthology*, ed. E. Ann Kaplan (Frederick, Md.: University Publications of America, 1983), 12–21.

CHAPTER ONE
"IN A CRISIS WE MUST HAVE A SENSE OF DRAMA":
CIVIL RIGHTS AND TELEVISUAL INFORMATION

1. José Muñoz, *Disidentifications: Queers of Color and the Performance of Politics* (Minneapolis: University of Minnesota Press, 1999), 182ff.

2. Thus the term "liveness" can be meaningfully deployed to denote kinds of television that are not *technically* live at all, but that promise something similar to what liveness promises: putatively immediate or transparent representation, perhaps, or a close temporal proximity to the event depicted. Network news coverage of civil rights movement activities, for example, were shot on film that was rushed by plane to New York for processing and editing. But such coverage still managed to claim to be more "real" than its print counterparts.

3. See, for example, the various epigraphs, all from King, to David Garrow's *Bearing the Cross: Martin Luther King, Jr., and the Southern Christian Leadership Conference* (New York: Vintage, 1988).

4. J. Fred MacDonald, *Blacks and White TV: African Americans in Television since 1948*, 2nd ed. (Chicago: Nelson Hall, 1992), 81.

5. See, for example, Harry S. Ashmore, *Hearts and Minds: The Anatomy of Racism from Roosevelt to Reagan* (New York: McGraw-Hill, 1982) and *Civil Rights and Wrongs: A Memoir of Race and Politics, 1944–1994* (New York: Pantheon, 1994); David Brinkley, *11 Presidents, 4 Wars, 22 Political Conventions, 1 Moon Landing, 3 Assassinations, 2,000 Weeks of News and Other Stuff on Television and 18 Years of Growing Up In North Carolina* (New York:

Knopf, 1995); Paul Good, *The Trouble I've Seen: White Journalist/Black Movement* (Washington, D.C.: Howard University Press, 1975); Dan Rather and Mickey Herskowitz, *The Camera Never Blinks: Adventures of a TV Journalist* (New York: William Morrow, 1977); and Howard K. Smith, *Events Leading up to My Death: The Life of a Twentieth Century Reporter* (New York: St. Martin's, 1996).

6. Reuven Frank, *Out of Thin Air: The Brief Wonderful Life of Network News* (New York: Simon & Schuster, 1991).

7. Ibid., 7.

8. Ibid., 21.

9. Harry Reasoner apparently shares Frank's sentiment (though he disagrees with his periodization). He is quoted by Ashmore in *Hearts and Minds* as saying that Little Rock was "where television came to influence, if not to maturity" (269).

10. Frank, *Thin Air*, 41; original emphasis.

11. Ibid., 50.

12. Ibid., 94.

13. Michael Curtin, *Redeeming the Wasteland: Television Documentary and Cold War Politics* (New Brunswick: Rutgers University Press, 1995), 177–96.

14. John Lewis, with Michael D'Orso, *Walking with the Wind: A Memoir of the Movement* (New York: Simon & Schuster, 1998), 267–68.

15. Good, *The Trouble I've Seen*, 95.

16. On the southern tendency to scapegoat the press, see Good, *The Trouble I've Seen*, 53; Robert Patterson, founder of the Citizen's Council, interviewed in Howell Raines, *My Soul Is Rested: Movement Days in the Deep South Remembered* (New York: Penguin, 1983), 297–303; Lewis, *Walking with the Wind*, 111. Violence against journalists in the South during the civil rights movement has been widely documented. See, for example, Adam Fairclough, *To Redeem the Soul of America: The Southern Christian Leadership Conference and Martin Luther King, Jr.* (Athens: University of Georgia Press, 1987), 240; David Halberstam, *The Children* (New York: Random House, 1998), 503; Thomas C. Leonard, "Antislavery, Civil Rights, and Incendiary Material," in *Media and Revolution: Comparative Perspectives*, ed. Jeremy D. Popkin, Jr. (Lexington: University Press of Kentucky, 1995), 115–35; Lewis, *Walking with the Wind*, 158, 268; the various journalists interviewed by Raines in *My Soul Is Rested*; Rather and Herskowitz, *The Camera Never Blinks*, 74ff.; Reese Schonfeld, "The Unsung Heroes of TV News," *Channels* (March/April 1983); Andrew Young, *An Easy Burden: The Civil Rights Movement and the Transformation of America* (New York: HarperCollins, 1996), 293.

17. Smith, *Events*, 269–70 (emphasis added).

18. Ibid., 271.

19. Ibid., 275.

20. Ibid., 283ff. See as well the transcript for Smith's *News and Comment* of 26 May 1963, Shuttlesworth, KLA, box 3, folder 8.

21. Taylor Branch, *Parting the Waters: America in the King Years, 1954–1963* (New York: Simon & Schuster, 1988), 223.

22. Leonard, "Antislavery, Civil Rights, and Incendiary Material," 125–26.

23. Frank, *Thin Air*, 124.

24. Daniel Schorr, quoted in David Halberstam, *The Fifties* (New York: Villard, 1993), 679.

25. For information on the licensing of television stations by state, see "Communications," *Statistical Abstracts of the United States* (Washington, D.C.: GPO, 1948–60); for information on the percentages of homes with television sets broken down by region, see U.S. Bureau of the Census, *Housing and Construction Reports*, Series H-121 (Washington, D.C.: GPO, 1955–60).

26. William Boddy, *Fifties Television: The Medium and Its Critics* (Urbana and Chicago: University of Illinois Press, 1990), 42–62.

27. In *Blacks and White TV*, MacDonald, states that "[g]iven the freeze on licensing new stations by the Federal Communications Commission, not until 1953 was the South able to redress this imbalance. Until that date, there were no operative TV transmitters in Mississippi, Arkansas, or South Carolina" (74). Steven Classen, in "Broadcast Law and Segregation: A Social History of the WLBT Case" (Ph.D. diss., University of Wisconsin, Madison, 1995), confirms MacDonald's dates, listing January 1953 as the date that Mississippi's first station, WJTV in Jackson, went on-air, with the infamous WBLT going on-air in December 1953. *Statistical Abstracts of the United States*, however, indicates that Mississippi and South Carolina had no stations in 1953, and four and nine respectively in 1955. Inexplicably, *Statistical Abstracts* contains no data for 1954.

28. My discussion of "the economics of networking" here is heavily indebted to Boddy's chapter of the same name in *Fifties Television*, 113–31.

29. MacDonald identifies an early "promise" on the part of the early television industry to be "bias-free" and argues that television reneged on this promise in part because of the growth of southern audiences. While I read early industry policy-statements on race rather more suspiciously than MacDonald does, I agree that the penetration of television into the deep South necessitated a renegotiation of earlier representational conventions. See *Blacks in White TV*, chapters 1 and 6.

30. MacDonald, *Blacks and White TV*, 68, 82.

31. Transcript of Howard K. Smith's *News and Comment*, 26 May 1963, Shuttlesworth, KLA, box 3, folder 8. Morgan refers here to three well-known civil rights documentaries: ABC's "Walk in My Shoes," *Bell and Howell Close-Up* 19 September 1961 (in the collections at MTR and UCLA); "Who Speaks for the South?" *CBS Reports* 27 May 1960; and "Sit-In," *NBC White Paper*, 20 December 1960 (MBC). I will discuss "Sit-In" at length in the next chapter.

32. Classen, "Broadcast Law and Segregation," 88.

33. John Chancellor, quoted in David Halberstam, *The Children*, 489. Frank confirms Chancellor's recollection: "Some NBC affiliates in the South chose not to carry us at all, believing, but never saying, that the New York-based networks were in favor of integration. We were particularly suspect because of all those stories on *Outlook*. The grapevine quoted jokes about the Nigger Broadcasting Company" (*Thin Air*, 117).

34. Indeed, we might see the controversial series, *The Gray Ghost*, the story

of a Confederate general, which debuted during the Little Rock crisis in 1957, as an index of these conflicting desires.

35. I am indebted here to Thomas C. Leonard's assertion, in "Antislavery, Civil Rights and Incendiary Material," that "when media play a role in revolution, the reason is often that leaders manage to force new readings of news and draw legitimacy for these interpretations. . . . [W]ords and pictures that once seemed safe become infuriating in a new context" (115).

36. Raines, interview with Ruby Hurley, *My Soul is Rested*, 136.

37. Young, *An Easy Burden*, 303. For a fascinating and detailed account of SNCC's efforts to maintain the press's attention during Freedom Summer, see Mary King, *Freedom Song: A Personal Story of the 1960s Civil Rights Movement*, 1st ed. (New York: Morrow, 1987).

38. Interview with Albert Turner, in Raines, *My Soul is Rested*, 189.

39. Interview with Willie Bolden, ibid., 193.

40. Fairclough, *To Redeem the Soul of America*, 8

41. On local campaigns against racist broadcasters, the best source is Classen, "Broadcast Law and Segregation," though the efforts he discusses were not led by SNCC. For clues to SNCC's media strategy, see King, *Freedom Song*, as well as the various policy statements on communications in the SNCC records, KLA: "Toward a Theory for Communications," box 24, folder "Communications Department n.d."; "Radio and Television Programming and Editorializing," box 33, folder "Correspondence, n.d."; "Press Procedures," box 36, folder "Staff Memos 1964"; "Memo to SNCC Field Staff re Efficient Press System," box 36, folder "Staff Memos 1964"; "A Story About SNCC Communications," box 153, folder 8.

42. Garrow, *Bearing the Cross*, 23. On the Montgomery movement, see also Stewart Burns, *Daybreak of Freedom: The Montgomery Bus Boycott* (Chapel Hill: University of North Carolina Press, 1997); David Garrow, ed., *The Walking City: The Montgomery Bus Boycott, 1955–1956* (Brooklyn: Carlson, 1989); Jo Ann Gibson Robinson, *The Montgomery Bus Boycott and the Women Who Started It: The Memoir of Jo Ann Gibson Robinson* (Knoxville: University of Tennessee Press, 1987); and Roberta Hughes Wright, *The Birth of the Montgomery Bus Boycott* (Southfield, Mich.: Charro, 1991).

43. The standard account of the Till lynching and its aftermath is Stephen J. Whitfield's *A Death in the Delta: The Story of Emmett Till* (Baltimore: Johns Hopkins University Press, 1991). For an extremely useful discussion of the visuality of the Till case, see Jacqueline Goldsby, "The High and Low Tech of It: The Meaning of Lynching and the Death of Emmett Till," *Yale Journal of Criticism* 9, no. 2 (1996): 245–82.

44. The latter point is crucial. As Leonard points out, southerners made their own images—lynching photography—but as long as those photographs circulated only within racist communities they had no incendiary value for blacks. Such images must be taken out of the context in which they exemplify a kind of racial common sense in order to signify progressively ("Antislavery, Civil Rights, and Incendiary Material," 125). On the role of visuality in the Till case and in 1950s culture generally, see also Goldsby, "The High and Low Tech of It."

45. Halberstam, *The Fifties*, 440–41.

46. Garrow, *Bearing the Cross*, 19–20.

47. Halberstam, *The Fifties*, 559.

48. Ibid., 561–62.

49. Garrow notes that press comparisons of King to Gandhi began quite early in the boycott; these would have enabled the framing of the events in Montgomery as "international" (*Bearing the Cross*, 66).

50. On the blacking out of movement coverage by local newspapers in the South, see Halberstam, *The Fifties*, 557ff; interview with Ed Gardner in Raines, *My Soul Is Rested*, 139–45.

51. Fairclough, *To Redeem the Soul of America*, 18.

52. See, for example, Robert J. Donovan and Ray Scherer, *Unsilent Revolution: Television News and American Public Life, 1948–1991* (Cambridge: Cambridge University Press, 1992), 15; Fairclough, *To Redeem the Soul of America*, 28.

53. In regard to the television show, Branch quotes a letter from Stanley Levinson to King: "All we need is a sponsor to give us a half hour weekly. We already have the star" (*Parting the Waters*, 225). King quoted in Garrow, *Bearing the Cross*, 97.

54. On the Birmingham campaign, see Glenn T. Eskew, *But for Birmingham: The Local and National Movements in the Civil Rights Struggle* (Chapel Hill: University of North Carolina Press, 1997); Andrew Michael Manis, *A Fire You Can't Put Out: The Civil Rights Life of Birmingham's Reverend Fred Shuttlesworth* (Tuscaloosa: University of Alabama Press, 1999); and William A. Nunnelley, *Bull Connor* (Tuscaloosa: University of Alabama Press, 1991).

55. Young, *An Easy Burden*, 226.

56. Fairclough, *To Redeem the Soul of America*, 126.

57. Young, *An Easy Burden*, 111–12.

58. Ibid., 207.

59. Fairclough, *To Redeem the Soul of America*, 122; Garrow, *Bearing the Cross*, 247.

60. Fairclough, *To Redeem the Soul of America*, 123; Branch, *Parting the Waters*, 736; Garrow, *Bearing the Cross*, 244–45

61. The phrase "infantile citizenship" is Lauren Berlant's. For a rich account of the vicissitudes of the infantile citizen, see her *The Queen of America Goes to Washington City: Essays on Sex and Citizenship* (Durham: Duke University Press, 1997).

62. David Garrow, *Protest at Selma: Martin Luther King, Jr., and the Voting Rights Act of 1965* (New Haven: Yale University Press, 1978), 227, 226.

63. On the Selma movement, see J. L. Chestnut, Jr., *Black in Selma: The Uncommon Life of J. L. Chestnut, Jr.* (New York: Farrar, Straus and Giroux, 1990); Charles E. Fager, *Selma, 1965* (New York: Scribner, 1974); Stephen L. Longenecker, *Selma's Peacemaker: Ralph Smeltzer and Civil Rights Mediation* (Philadelphia: Temple University Press, 1987); Mary Stanton, *From Selma to Sorrow: The Life and Death of Viola Liuzzo* (Athens: University of Georgia Press, 1998); and Sheyann Webb et al., *Selma, Lord, Selma: Girlhood Memories of the Civil Rights Days* (Tuscaloosa: University of Alabama Press, 1980).

64. Halberstam, *The Children*, 487, 490. See also Fager, *Selma, 1965*, 34.

65. Young, quoted in Fairclough, *To Redeem the Soul of America*, 226–27.

66. Fager, *Selma, 1965*, 31; Garrow, *Bearing the Cross*, 379; Fairclough, *To Redeem the Soul of America*, 230.

67. Lewis, *Walking With the Wind*, 310; compare with Fager, *Selma, 1965*, 33.

68. Accounts differ as to whether Clark was initiated into the Dallas County Voter's League or the SCLC. See Fager, *Selma, 1965*, 34; Garrow, *Bearing the Cross*, 379.

69. Garrow, *Bearing the Cross*, 383.

70. King's notes made in Selma Jail, 1–5 February 1965, MLK, KLA, Box 22, Folder 6.

71. My account of this incident is based on Fager, *Selma, 1965*, 70; Halberstam, *The Children* 501–2; Garrow, *Bearing the Cross*, 391; and "1965: Bridge to Freedom," *Eyes on the Prize: America's Civil Rights Years* (Turner Home Entertainment/PBS Home Video, 1995). Because of the difficulty of gaining access to tapes and images from network archives, the images of Selma in this chapter have been taken from *Eyes on the Prize*.

72. Fager, *Selma, 1965*, 70.

73. Fairclough, *To Redeem the Soul of America*, 237. In *Bearing the Cross*, King biographer David Garrow writes, "Only years later did Vivian admit that it was one of Clark's deputies who had punched him. 'Clark didn't, but he wanted to take credit for it,' and Vivian had no reason to contest it. 'He was the symbol, not the guy standing beside him'"(391). Later accounts of the incident (Fairclough, Halberstam) have returned to the earlier version of the story; I have done so based on my viewing of some of the news footage, which indicates quite clearly, I think, that it was Clark who hit Vivian.

74. Fager, *Selma, 1965*, 70.

75. Fager, *Selma, 1965*, 98; Garrow, *Bearing the Cross*, 399; Lewis, *Walking With the Wind*, 331; Young, *An Easy Burden*, 358. Fairclough notes, "Many of the clergymen [who came to participate in the Selma to Montgomery march] were old supporters of the civil rights movement, but most, like the scores of lay people present, had traveled to Selma on impulse after viewing the graphic television film of the attack on Pettus Bridge" (*To Redeem the Soul of America*, 243).

76. See Halberstam, *The Children*, 516, and Lewis, *Walking With the Wind*, 337.

77. Halberstam, *The Children*, 515.

78. Nelson Benton, quoted in Raines, *My Soul is Rested*, 386.

79. Young, *An Easy Burden*, 358.

80. Benton, quoted in Raines, *My Soul is Rested*, 386.

81. George B. Leonard, quoted in Garrow, *Protest at Selma*, 84.

82. Mary Ann Doane, "Information, Crisis, Catastrophe," in *Logics of Television*, ed. Patricia Mellencamp (Bloomington: Indiana University Press, 1990), 235–38.

CHAPTER TWO
THE DOUBLE LIFE OF "SIT-IN"

1. During the seasons from 1959–60 to 1963–64, the following civil rights documentaries aired on *CBS Reports*: "Who Speaks for the South?" 27 May 1960; "Who Speaks for Birmingham?" May 18, 1961 (available at MTR); "Mississippi and the Fifteenth Amendment," September 26, 1962; "The Other Face of Dixie," October 24, 1962; "The Harlem Temper," December 11, 1963 (MTR); and "Filibuster: Birth Struggle of a Law," March 18, 1964 (MTR). *The NBC White Paper* series included "Sit-In," December 20, 1960 (MBC) and "Adam Clayton Powell," March 12, 1964. Civil rights documentaries in the *Bell and Howell Close-Up* series on ABC "Cast the First Stone," September 27, 1960 (MBC and MTR); "The Children Were Watching," February 16, 1961; and "Walk in My Shoes," September 19, 1961 (MTR and UCLA). Documentary specials airing during this period include NBC's "The American Revolution of 1963," September 2, 1963 (LOC); NBC's "Crisis: Behind a Presidential Commitment," October 21, 1963 (MBC, MTR, UCLA); and NET's "Take This Hammer," with James Baldwin, February 1964 (LOC). This listing includes only nationally aired documentaries, and thus omits the many locally produced civil rights documentaries that aired all over the country. A good selection of these is available at MBC.

2. I am heavily indebted, here and in the next paragraph, to the following sources: Christopher Anderson, *Hollywood TV: The Studio System in the Fifties*, 1st ed., Texas Film Studies Series (Austin: University of Texas Press, 1994); William Boddy, *Fifties Television: The Medium and Its Critics* (Urbana and Chicago: University of Illinois Press, 1990); and Michael Curtin, *Redeeming the Wasteland: Television Documentary and Cold War Politics* (New Brunswick: Rutgers University Press, 1995).

3. Curtin, *Redeeming the Wasteland*, 69.

4. On Minow, see ibid., 24–27 and 32–34; see also Mary Ann Watson, *The Expanding Vista: American Television in the Kennedy Years* (Durham: Duke University Press, 1994), esp. chapter 1.

5. Curtin, *Redeeming the Wasteland*, 125.

6. It is not clear, in "Sit-In," what the console Huntley sits in front of is, but Curtin identifies it in his extensive discussion of "Panama: Danger Zone," the documentary that immediately followed "Sit-In" in the *NBC White Paper* series. Curtin characterizes Huntley in "Panama: Danger Zone" as "seated at a control console, dressed in a business suit, and speaking authoritatively into the camera. He assumes a seemingly neutral, omniscient stance in relation to the filmed images and delivers information in brief, declarative phrases." (*Redeeming the Wasteland*, 200). The placement of Huntley in the control room seems to me to be an obvious allusion to Edward R. Murrow's similar placement in *See It Now* (CBS, 1951–58). The framing of this shot thus seeks to borrow Murrow's prestige for Huntley. But in *See It Now*, Murrow's position in the control room was linked visually and directly to the television apparatus via the presence of monitors and other equipment in the shot, as in the famous episode in which viewers were treated to a split screen displaying simultaneous live shots

of both the Brooklyn Bridge and the Golden Gate Bridge. In Huntley's studio, though, the objects of the controls (monitors and other apparatus) have disappeared. These shots thus offer Huntley a "control" more generalized and less specific than Murrow's.

7. Maureen Turim, *Flashbacks in Film: Memory & History* (New York: Routledge, 1989), 1.

8. Stunningly, "Sit-In" identifies none of the African Americans who appear in the documentary (many of the whites are identified in voice-over by Huntley, or they introduce themselves). I have identified Angeline Butler from a picture in David Halberstam's *The Children* (New York: Random House, 1998), an account of the Nashville movement and of the later histories of several of its key participants (on LaPrad in particular, see 58–59, 129–133, and 703). It is worth noting, though, that Halberstam himself never mentions "Sit-In," which is remarkable, given both the documentary's later life in the movement and his interest — in *The Fifties* (New York: Villard, 1993) and later in *The Children* — on the effects of television coverage on racial struggles of the 1960s. I attribute this to Halberstam's desire to cast Nashville as a media scene dominated by print; Halberstam himself was a reporter at the *Nashville Tennessean* during the heyday of the Nashville movement.

9. Turim, *Flashbacks in Film*, 2.

10. Curtin, *Redeeming the Wasteland*, 187.

11. Turim, *Flashbacks in Film*, 27.

12. Most integrationist whites and activist blacks, on the other hand, are shot in respectful medium shots or medium close-ups, which imply an appropriate distance from the camera and a seemly perspective on the matters at hand.

13. Andrew Young, *A Way Out of No Way: The Spiritual Memoirs of Andrew Young* (Nashville: Nelson, 1994), 49.

14. *An Easy Burden: The Civil Rights Movement and the Transformation of America* (New York: HarperCollins, 1996), 124–29.

15. Ibid., 125. A number of the sources I will discuss here suggest that "Sit-In" was commonly called "The Nashville Sit-In Story" within the civil rights movement. Young's discussion is sufficiently detailed, though, as to allay any doubts that he and I are talking about the same text.

16. Young, *An Easy Burden*, 126.

17. Ibid., 127.

18. Ibid., 145.

19. Ibid., 143.

20. Letter from Fred Halsted to SNCC, 26 December 1961, SNCC, KLA, Box 24, folder "Communications Department, n.d."

21. Letter from SNCC office to Fred Halsted, 3 January 1962, SNCC, KLA, Box 24, folder "Communications Department, n.d."

22. Halberstam, *The Children*, 387–95.

23. Taylor Branch, *Parting the Waters: America in the King Years, 1954–1963* (New York: Simon & Schuster, 1988), p. 752 and *Pillar of Fire: American in the King Years, 1963–65* (New York: Simon & Schuster, 1998), 76, 559; Adam Fairclough, *To Redeem the Soul of America: The Southern Christian Leadership Conference and Martin Luther King, Jr.* (Athens: University of Geor-

gia Press, 1987), 230; John Lewis with Michael D'Orso, *Walking with the Wind: A Memoir of the Movement* (New York: Simon & Schuster, 1998), 196; Young, *An Easy Burden*, 236.

24. Curtin, *Redeeming the Wasteland*, 227.

25. Curtin, *Redeeming the Wasteland*, 228.

26. Thomas Cripps, *Making Movies Black: The Hollywood Message Movie from World War II to the Civil Rights Era* (New York: Oxford University Press, 1993); Donald Bogle, *Toms, Coons, Mulattoes, Mammies, and Bucks: An Interpretive History of Blacks in American Film*, new rev. ed. (New York: Continuum, 1991), 172.

27. These latter gestures were in fact repeated and amplified by the eventual rewriting of "Day-O" by movement singers to commemorate the Freedom Rides. Some of the lyrics are as follows:

> Freedom, give me freedom
> Freedom's coming and it won't be long
> Come Mr. Kennedy, take me out' my misery
> Freedom's coming and it won't be long
> Can't you see what segregation's doin' to me
> Freedom's coming and it won't be long
> Freedom, give me freedom
> Freedom's coming and it won't be long
> Oh I took a little ride on a Greyhound Bus,
> Freedom's coming and it won't be long
> to fight segregation 'cause I know we must.

See "Calypso Freedom," on the compact disc *Voices of the Civil Rights Movement: Black American Freedom Songs* (Washington: Smithsonian Folkways Recordings, 1997), track 6.

CHAPTER THREE
KING TV

1. Jane Feuer, "The Concept of Live Television: Ontology as Ideology," in *Regarding Television — Critical Approaches: An Anthology*, ed. E. Ann Kaplan (Frederick, Md.: University Publications of America, 1983).

2. Ibid., 13.

3. Ibid., 14.

4. Ibid., 14.

5. Ibid., 14.

6. I am indebted here to Todd Gitlin's work on hegemony and television. See, for example, *The Whole World Is Watching: Mass Media in the Making and Unmaking of the New Left* (Berkeley: University of California Press, 1980), esp. chapter 10.

7. Judith Butler, "Endangered/Endangering: Schematic Racism and White Paranoia," in *Reading Rodney King/Reading Urban Uprising*, ed. Robert Gooding-Williams (New York: Routledge, 1993), 17.

8. On direct address, see Margaret Morse's "Talk, Talk, Talk: The Space of

Discourse in Television News, Sportscasts, Talk Shows and Advertising," *Screen* 26 (1985): 2–15.

9. The helicopters-eye-view of South Central Los Angeles had by then been thoroughly linked, by national media culture generally and by Hollywood film in particular, to the gaze of the LAPD. Consider, for example, the deployment of helicopters within *Colors* (1988), *Boyz N the Hood* (1991), and *Grand Canyon* (1991).

10. Butler, "Endangered/Endangering," 21.

11. Rhonda Williams, "Accumulation as Evisceration: Urban Rebellion and the New Growth Dynamics," in *Reading Rodney King/Reading Urban Uprising*, 83. One of the many pleasures of Lynell George's chronicle of the rebellions, "Waiting for the Rainbow Sign," is the way in which it, as a streets-eye-view account, revises most of the assumptions and narrative conventions that have emerged in other representations of these events. See her *No Crystal Stair: African-Americans in the City of Angels* (New York: Verso, 1992), 9–16.

12. The most important consideration of these recombinatory practices is that of Todd Gitlin, in his *Inside Prime Time* (Berkeley: University of California Press, 2000).

13. What are we to make of the appearance of a character from *The Simpsons*, one of Fox's most successful, durable and visible series, embedded in an NBC program? I would suggest that this intertextual reference does more than simply promote television per se, as Mimi White argues in her article about such cross-network references, "Crossing Wavelengths: The Diegetic and Referential Imaginary of American Commercial Television," *Cinema Journal* 25, no. 2 (Winter 1986): 51–64. *The Simpsons* after all, marked Fox as a new threat to the dominance of the big three networks when Fox programmed it against NBC's enormously successful *The Cosby Show* in 1990, and it has, of course, outlasted both *The Cosby Show* and *L.A. Law* itself. Thus I argue that "Homer Simpson" functions here as the sign that allows this text both to register and to struggle against its own network's increasingly obsolete programming strategies and demographic self-understanding. I will return to these points in the section on *Doogie Howser*.

14. I am indebted for this point to Butler's suggestion that King's "body . . . received [the officers'] blows in return for the ones it was about to deliver, the blows which were that body in its essential gestures, even as the one gesture that body can be seen to make is to raise its palm outward to stave off the blows against it. According to this racist episteme, he is hit in exchange for the blows he never delivered, but which he is always, by virtue of his blackness, always about to deliver" ("Endangered/Endangering," 19).

15. Here I am relying on the testimony of California Highway Patrol officer Melanie Singer, in the Simi Valley trial: "At that time, I withdrew my weapon, pointed it at the suspect and told him to get his hand away from his butt—I could not see where his hand was—and at that time he turned his . . . body around to where his rear end was facing me. He grabbed his right buttock with his right hand and shook it at me." See *The "Rodney King" Case: What the Jury Saw in California v. Powell*, Court TV compilation tape of the Simi Valley trial, 1992. Though Singer's testimony might lead us to assume that King's ges-

ture was directed at Singer and thus heterosexually motivated, I think such a supposition would be a mistake, as Singer's irrelevance to the proceedings was adequately established by the Simi Valley trial. Rather I propose to read King's gesture as addressed to and received by Singer together with the other officers, all of whom were men.

16. Stephen Heath, "Representing Television," in *Logics of Television*, ed. Patricia Mellencamp (Bloomington: Indiana University Press), 270.

17. Mary Anne Doane, "Information, Crisis, Catastrophe," in *Logics of Television*, 233.

CHAPTER FOUR
GIULIANI TIME: URBAN POLICING AND *BROOKLYN SOUTH*

1. This essay was completed before 9/11/01. I have chosen not to discuss Giuliani's response to the World Trade Center bombings or the reception of that response.

2. See, for example, John Tierney, "The Big City: No One Wants to See Crime In a Tradeoff," *New York Times*, March 25, 1999, B1, and Frank Bruni, "Ideas & Trends: Crimes of the War on Crime," *New York Times*, February 21, 1999, sec. 4, p. 1. Bruni notes, "Many Americans have tacitly blessed a more vigorous, invasive, belligerent brand of policing."

3. Judith Grant, "Prime Time Crime: Television Portrayals of Law Enforcement," *Journal of American Culture* 15, no. 1 (1992): 58.

4. For an essay that takes up similar questions in the British context, see Charlotte Brunsdon, "Structure of Anxiety: Recent British Television Crime Fiction," *Screen* 39, no. 3 (1998): 223–43.

5. On the show's (and particularly the pilot's) violence, see Bill Carter, "TV Notes," *New York Times*, July 16, 1997, C18; Gail Shister, "Reshoot of Bochco's 'Brooklyn South' pilot will add a black officer," *Philadelphia Inquirer*, July 16, 1997; Monica Collins, "'Brooklyn' Accents True — Bochco Touch Equals Quality," *Boston Herald*, September 22, 1997, p. 34; Dennis Byrne, "Stereotypical Reality," *Chicago Sun-Times*, September 24, 1997, p. 43; Matthew Gilbert, "Another Badge of Honor: 'Brooklyn South' Engaging, Gimickless," *Boston Globe*, September 22, 1997, C6; Caryn James, "When the Thin Blue Line Becomes Unstrung," *New York Times*, September 22, 1997, E1; Eric Mink, "A Rookie Explodes onto the Scene," *Daily News*, September 22, 1997, p. 64; Virginia Rohan, "Into the Wild Blue Yonder: Bochco's New Cop Drama, Brooklyn South, Takes TV Violence to the Limit," *Bergen Record*, September 22 1997, Y1. On its "authenticity," see Collins, "'Brooklyn' Accent's True"; and Verne Gay, "A Serious Shoot-Em Up," *Newsday*, September 22, 1997, B6. On the echoes of the Louima case, see Gilbert, "Another Badge"; James, "Thin Blue Line"; Rohan, "Wild Blue Yonder"; and Greg Braxton and Jane Hall, "Too Close to Reality?" *Los Angeles Times*, August 21, 1997, F50.

6. The officers alleged to have been involved only in the beating on the way to the station house, Thomas Wiese and Thomas Bruder, were acquitted, though at the time of this writing they are still facing federal charges of obstruction of

justice. After several fellow officers testified against him, Justin Volpe pled guilty to violating Louima's civil rights. Charles Schwartz was also found guilty.

7. Dan Barry, "Charges of Brutality: The Overview," *New York Times*, August 15, 1997, A1; ABC News, *Nightline*, "The Blue Wall," August 22, 1997.

8. *Nightline*, "The Blue Wall."

9. John Kifner, "Louima Says His Attackers Did Not Yell 'Giuliani Time,'" *New York Times*, January 15, 1998, B3; Joseph P. Fried, "In Louima's First Day on Stand, He Tells of Brutal Police Assault," *New York Times*, May 7, 1999, A1.

10. John Kifner, "Louima Says His Attackers Did Not Yell 'Giuliani Time,'" B3; Joseph P. Fried, "In Louima's First Day on Stand, He Tells of Brutal Police Assault," *New York Times*, May 7, 1999, A1.

11. For a wonderfully passionate and appropriately horrifying account of Giuliani Time, particularly as it affects the city's poorest citizens, see Neil Smith, "Giuliani Time: The Revanchist 1990s," *Social Text* 16, no. 4 (1998): 1–20.

12. Wayne Barrett, "50 Reasons to Loathe Your Mayor," *Village Voice*, November 4, 1997. Reason #1: "Saying it would be 'a good thing' if poor people left the city. RG said in response to questions about the effect of his welfare cuts: 'That's not an unspoken part of our strategy. That is our strategy.' Though this comment was reported by the news director of the city's own television station, the mayor corrected it, saying an exodus 'could be a natural consequence,' though 'not the intention of our policy.' The mayor's favorite newspaper, the *Post*, cited one of RG's 'chief policy architects' as saying: 'The poor will eventually figure out that it's a lot easier to be homeless where it's warm.'"

13. My thinking about the politics of the new Times Square is indebted to Samuel R. Delany, *Times Square Red, Times Square Blue* (New York: New York University Press, 1999).

14. See David Kocieniewski, "The 1997 Elections: Crime; Mayor Gets Credit for a Safer City, but Wider Trends Play a Role," *New York Times*, October 28, 1997, B4.

15. Delany, *Times Square Red, Times Square Blue*, 158ff.

16. Wayne Barrett, "Beating the Cops," *Village Voice*, December 23, 1997, 36; Nat Hentoff, "Jim Crow in Blue: Eighty Per Cent of Civilian Complaints are from Nonwhites," *The Village Voice*, September 23, 1997; Deborah Sontag and Dan Barry, "Challenge to Authority: A Special Report," *New York Times*, November 19, 1997, A1.

17. The Amnesty International Report, "Police brutality and excessive force in the New York City Police Department," can be found on the World Wide Web at http://www.amnesty.org/ailib/aipub/1996/AMR/25103696.htm. For press coverage of the report, see Clifford Krauss, "Rights Group Finds Abuse of Suspects by City Police," *New York Times*, June 26, 1996, B4, and Ellis Henican, "Please and May I Joining the Finest," *Newsday*, June 27, 1996, A2.

18. Deborah Sontag and Dan Barry, "The Price of Brutality: A Special Report," *New York Times*, September 17, 1997, A1; Deborah Sontag and Dan Barry, "Challenge to Authority," A1; Wayne Barrett, "Beating the Cops," 36; Kevin Flynn, "How to Sue the Police (and Win): Lawyers Share Trade Secrets of a Growth Industry," *New York Times*, October 2, 1999, B1.

19. Dan Barry, "Giuliani Dismisses Police Proposals by His Task Force," *New York Times*, March 27, 1998, A1. The group's recommendations included instituting residency requirements for police officers, tougher entrance requirements for the police academy, and ending the "48 hour rule," which forces investigators to wait forty-eight hours before questioning officers who may have committed a crime. See also Barry, "Giuliani Sneers, and Even Friends Bridle," *New York Times*, March 28, 1998, A1; and "Giuliani Concedes He Could Have Been More Gracious," *New York Times*, April 2, 1998, B5.

20. Alison Mitchell, "Corruption in Uniform: The Mayor," *New York Times*, July 8, 1994, A1.

21. Clifford Krauss, "Corruption in Uniform: The Overview," *New York Times*, July 7, 1994, A1.

22. Krauss, "Corruption in Uniform."

23. David Kocieniewski, "Giuliani Cool to Independent Police Monitors," *Newsday*, July 8, 1994, A20.

24. Selwyn Raab, "New York's Police Allow Corruption, Mollen Panel Says," *New York Times*, December 29, 1993, A1.

25. David Kocieniewski, "Corruption Panel Courts Giuliani," *Newsday*, November 19, 1993, 38.

26. Jonathan Larsen, "Prescription for Police Corruption Draws Controversy," United Press International, December 28, 1993.

27. Selwyn Raab, "Mollen Panel to Recommend Permanent Corruption Body," *New York Times*, December 29, 1993, B1.

28. David Kocieniewski, "Corruption Panel Courts Giuliani," 38.

29. Kocieniewski writes, "Giuliani, a former federal prosecutor who tried several cases against corrupt officers during the Knapp Commission scandal, said he will urge Gov. Mario Cuomo to revive the Special State Prosecutor's Office disbanded in 1990. Giuliani conceded it was 'highly unlikely' Cuomo would make such a move during an election year" ("Giuliani Cool to Independent Police Monitors," A20). See also Bob Liff and David Kocieniewski, "Rudy Backs New Cop Monitor," *Newsday*, August 20 1994, A06, which states, "Although Giuliani favors the creation of a legislatively mandated special prosecutor's office to investigate and try crooked officers, Gov. Mario Cuomo has indicated that he wouldn't authorize such a move."

30. Patricia Cohen, "Surprise! Rudy Backs the Panel," *Newsday*, April 21, 1994, A04.

31. David Kocieniewski and George E. Jordan, "Giuliani's Police Monitor: Will Watchdog Have Teeth?," *Newsday*, April 29, 1994, A06.

32. Alison Mitchell, "Corruption in Uniform," A1.

33. "Giuliani Supports Police Monitor," *New York Times* August 20, 1994, A1.

34. See John Shanahan, "Independent Police Review Nears Reality," *Bergen Record*, October 27, 1994, C14; Jonathan P. Hicks, "2 Council Committees Pass Bill to Create Police Agency," *New York Times*, October 27, 1994, B3; Hicks, "Giuliani Expected to Veto Police Monitor Bill," *New York Times*, December 12, 1994, B3; and Bob Liff, "Rudy's Power Play: He Starts Own Corruption Panel," *Newsday*, February 28, 1995, A17.

35. See Clifford Krauss, "Police Investigating Corruption Charges at Bronx Precinct," *New York Times*, February 2, 1995, A1; Clifford Krauss and Adam Nositter, "Crossing the Line — A Special Report: Bronx Abuse Stirs Crackdown on Police," *New York Times*, May 2, 1995, A1; Krauss, "16 Police Officers Are Indicted in Bronx Precinct Graft Inquiry," *New York Times*, May 3, 1995, A1; and Clifford Krauss, "16 Officers Indicted in a Pattern of Brutality in a Bronx Precinct," *New York Times*, May 4, 1995.

36. Jonathan P. Hicks, "Giuliani Considers Creating Own Police-Monitor Panel," *New York Times*, February 1, 1995, B3. Hicks writes, "Paul A. Crotty, the Mayor's Corporation Counsel, said the administration was drawing up plans for an agency to serve at the Mayor's pleasure."

37. Bob Liff, "Rudy's Power Play." See also Jonathan P. Hicks, "Giuliani Names His Own Panel to Monitor Police Corruption," *New York Times*, February 28, 1995, B1. The mayor's legal action against the council was eventually upheld by the State Supreme Court. See Daniel Wise, "City Council's Board on Police Invalidated: Mayor Wins Clear Victory in Power Struggle," *New York Law Journal* (July 29, 1995): 1.

38. William K. Rashbaum, "Getting Back in Line: Rudy Unveils Plan to Stem Cop Corruption," *Newsday*, June 15, 1995, p. 5; George James, "New York Calls for Precincts to Control Police Monitoring," *New York Times*, June 15, 1995, A1.

39. Rashbaum, "Getting Back in Line, p. 5; George James, "New York Calls for Precincts to Control Police Monitoring," A1.

40. Jonathan P. Hicks, "Judge Invalidates Creation of Police Corruption Panel," *New York Times*, June 29, 1995, B3. This decision was upheld on appeal; see Clifford J. Levy, "Mayor's Veto of New Panel on Police is Upheld," *New York Times*, January 11, 1997, sect. 1, p. 29.

41. George James, "Mayoral Commission Offers Qualified Praise on Police Anti-Corruption Drive," *New York Times*, March 30, 1996, sect. 1, p. 26; David Kocieniewski, "Mayor's Panel on Corruption Faces Scrutiny," *New York Times*, September 22, 1997, B1. Kocieniewski quotes a commission staff member as saying that "[the commission's reports] are so sanitized by the Mayor's office it got to be a joke."

42. Vivian S. Toy, "Council Backs a New Police Review Board," *New York Times*, October 1, 1997, B2; Toy, "Giuliani Again Vetoes Bill for Outside Police Monitor," *New York Times*, October 31, 1997, B3; Toy, "Veto of Police Board Overridden," *New York Times*, November 26, 1997, B3; Norimitsu Onishi, "Giuliani Sues To Block Police Board," *New York Times*, March 26, 1998, B7. The City Council's veto was eventually upheld by New York's State Supreme Court. See David Rohde, "Judge Rules for New Board To Fight Police Corruption," *New York Times*, September 1, 1999, B3.

43. Michael Cooper, "Mayor to Help Police Monitor He Had Fought," *New York Times*, September 17, 1997, B1.

44. My thinking here is indebted to the work of Lauren Berlant and Michael Warner. See in particular Berlant's "National Brands/National Body: *Imitation of Life*," and Warner's "The Mass Public and the Mass Subject," both in *The Phantom Public Sphere*, ed. Bruce Robbins (Minneapolis: University of Minnesota Press, 1993), 173–209 and 234–57.

45. The indispensable article on how television does this through narrative structure is Judith Mayne, "*L.A. Law* and Prime-Time Feminism," *Discourse* X, no. 2 (1988): 30–47.

46. I have gathered anecdotal evidence for this conclusion every time I've given a version of this essay as a lecture. Audience members at my talks have invariably confessed that they tried to watch the show, but gave up when they found the main characters—the clean-cut, handsome, thirtysomething white men who populate the imaginary 74th precinct—indistinguishable from one another. "I couldn't tell them apart," they would say, or, even better, "They all looked alike to me." I take this complaint about the show's visual register to be metaphorical for the show's paucity of identificatory possibilities.

47. Gail Shister, "Reshoot of Bochco's 'Brooklyn South' pilot will add a black officer," *Philadelphia Inquirer*, July 16, 1997.

48. Shister, "Reshoot." Gary Peller's "Race-Consciousness," in *Critical Race Theory: The Key Writings That Formed the Movement*, ed. Kimberlé Creshaw, Neil Gotanda, Gary Peller, and Kendall Thomas (New York: New Press, 1995), 127–58, is useful in contextualizing the popular rhetoric of colorblindness Milch here invokes.

CHAPTER FIVE
CIVIL RIGHTS, DONE AND UNDONE

1. Greg Braxton, "NAACP will fight network TV lineups," *Los Angeles Times*, July 12, 1999, A1; and Lawrie Mifflin, "NAACP plans to press for more diverse TV shows," *New York Times*, July 13, 1999, A10.

2. Keith L. Alexander, "NAACP campaign changed more than TV group's political, economic power," *USA Today*, February 15, 2000, 3B, emphasis added.

3. Mark Mauer and Tracy Huling, *Young Black Americans and the Criminal Justice System* (Washington, D.C.: The Sentencing Project, 1994); *American Women: A Century of Change— What's Next?* (Washington, D.C.: The Women's Research and Education Institute, 1998).

4. See, for example, Michael A. Fletcher, "Once down, NAACP in fighting form," *Washington Post*, July 16, 1999, A03; Chrisena Coleman, "Revitalized NAACP," *Daily News*, July 18, 1999, 34; Sheryl McCarthy, "Mfume leads NAACP back into the nation's spotlight," *Baltimore Sun*, July 18, 1999, 3D; DeWayne Wickham, "TV network pacts boost ailing NAACP," *USA Today*, January 11, 2000, 15A.

5. Brian Lowry, "To increase diversity, NAACP may encourage TV network regulation," *Los Angeles Times*, January 27, 2000, F59.

6. The NAACP's 1915 campaign against D. W. Griffith's *Birth of a Nation*, for example, is detailed in Charles Flint Kellogg, *NAACP: A History of the National Association for the Advancement of Colored People*, vol. 1 (Baltimore: Johns Hopkins University Press, 1967), 142–45. On the organization's later campaign against *Amos 'n' Andy*, see Melvin Patrick Ely, *The Adventures of Amos 'n' Andy: A Social History of an American Phenomenon* (New York: Free Press, 1991), 213–44.

7. DeWayne Wickham, "NAACP smart to put squeeze on TV execs," *USA Today*, August 10, 1999, 15A. I am drawing here on Phillip Brian Harper's illuminating discussion of the complex relations between popular imaginations of the televisual image as a potential spur for social change, and the television industry as a potential source of black wealth, in "Extra Special Effects: Televisual Representation and the Claims of the 'Black Experience,'" in *Living Color: Race and Television in the United States*, ed. Sasha Torres (Durham: Duke University Press, 1998), 62–81.

8. The numbers for Latinos and Asian Americans were similarly shocking: eleven and three, respectively. See Greg Braxton, "Survey cites low number of minority writers on series," *Los Angeles Times*, October 9, 1999, F2.

9. Mfume quoted by Wendy J. Williams, "Minority actors: TV executives' new best friends," *Boston Herald*, September 3, 1999, S30. With respect to employment questions, the NAACP met with some initial success: by December, Mfume had parlayed the threat of boycotts and demonstrations into meetings with the CEOs of ABC, CBS, NBC, and Fox, and by January 2000 all four networks had "signed deals pledging to boost minority hiring in front of and behind the cameras, from their board rooms to their studios." See also Keith L. Alexander, "NAACP campaign."

10. Liz Leyden, "NAACP's Mfume warns of TV boycott," *Washington Post*, November 4, 1999, C07.

11. Braxton, "NAACP will fight network TV lineups."

12. Mike Adams, "Mfume takes up TV repair," *Baltimore Sun*, December 19, 1999, 1H.

13. Versions of this story of African Americans rushing to inform each other of a black presence on TV are to be found in, among other places, Elizabeth Alexander, "Today's News," in *The Venus Hottentot* (Charlottesville and London: University Press of Virginia, 1990), 51; Henry Louis Gates, Jr., *Colored People: A Memoir* (New York: Knopf, 1994), 22; bell hooks, *Yearning: Race, Gender and Cultural Politics* (Boston: South End, 1990), 3–4.

14. Erin Texeira, "TV networks accused of 'virtual whitewash,'" *Baltimore Sun*, July 13, 1999, 1A.

15. Mfume's program, *The Bottom Line*, is produced by WBAL-TV, Baltimore's NBC affiliate. CNN has aired *Both Sides with Jesse Jackson* since 1992. Henry Louis Gates's episode of the PBS documentary series *Frontline*, "The Two Nations of Black America," aired in 1998, while his PBS series, *The Wonders of the African World*, aired in 1999.

16. Adams, "Mfume takes up TV repair."

17. Herman Gray, "Remembering Civil Rights: Television Memory and the 1960s," in *The Revolution Wasn't Televised: Sixties Television and Social Conflict*, ed. Lynn Spigel and Michael Curtin (New York: Routledge, 1997), 148–58. I'm indebted here to Sharon Willis's discussion of race in contemporary police shows in *High Contrast: Race and Gender in Contemporary Hollywood Film* (Durham: Duke University Press, 1997), 5.

18. The cultural obsession with this pairing seems to me to be on the rise. One index of it may be James H. Cone, *Martin & Malcolm & America: A Dream or a Nightmare* (Maryknoll, N.Y.: Orbis, 1991). Another is certainly the

widespread reproduction of the photograph of their only meeting, which, of course, figures crucially in Spike Lee's *Do the Right Thing*, and is also used to illustrate Michael Eric Dyson's review of Cone's book. See "Martin and Malcolm," *Transition* 56 (1992): 48–59.

19. CBS, "The Harlem Temper," *CBS Reports*, December 18, 1963 (MTR); ABC, "Cast the First Stone," *Bell and Howell Close-Up*, September 27, 1960 (MBC, MTR).

20. Gray, "Remembering Civil Rights," 353, emphasis added.

21. Ibid., 356.

22. Lee quoted in Henry Louis Gates, Jr., "Generation X: A Conversation with Spike Lee and Henry Louis Gates," *Transition* 56 (1992): 184. See also Lee's chronicle of the film's production, *By Any Means Necessary: The Trials and Tribulations of the Making of* Malcolm X (New York: Hyperion, 1992).

23. On the gender politics of Malcolm X, see bell hooks, "Male Heroes and Female Sex Objects: Sexism in Spike Lee's *Malcolm X*," *Cineaste* 19, no. 4 (1993): 13–15.

24. Much of the text of the speech can be found in an interview with Malcolm X by Louis Lomax, in his *When the Word Is Given: A Report on Elijah Muhammad, Malcolm X and the Black Muslim World* (Cleveland and New York: World, 1963), 197–212.

25. See, for example "No Easy Walk (1961–63)," *Eyes on the Prize*, vol. 2, 1987 (distributed by PBS Home Video/Turner Home Entertainment).

26. The film here closely approximates some of Malcolm's actual TV appearances of the period. See, for example, the interview with Malcolm on the local Chicago public affairs program *City Desk*, March 1, 1963, MBC. On Malcolm's preparations for such appearances, see Ron Simmons and Marlon Riggs, "Sexuality, Television and Death: A Black Gay Dialogue on Malcolm X," in *Malcolm X in Our Own Image*, ed. Joe Wood (New York: St. Martin's, 1992), 135–54. As Riggs observes, "Malcolm used the media to address audiences that would be empowered by his message, even when the media was trying to define his message as being a threat to social order. In interviews, Malcolm was extremely analytical and piercing, thinking critically about how to respond to questions and avoid the pitfalls that would allow him to be portrayed as simply emotional or angry" (143). The script draws Malcolm's disquisition on the house Negro and the field Negro from Malcolm X's "Message to the Grass Roots," in *Malcolm X Speaks: Selected Speeches and Statements*, ed. George Breitman (New York: Pathfinder, 1993), 10–11. On the complexities of Malcolm's relation to the black bourgeoisie, whom he called "house Negroes," see Robin D. G. Kelley's "House Negroes on the Loose: Malcolm X and the Black Bourgeoisie," *Callaloo* 21, no. 2 (1998): 419–35.

27. I am indebted to Amanda Berry for this point, ample evidence for which is no doubt provided by Styles's assertion, after apprehending the knife-wielding Blake, that "a Beretta in the butt beats a Bowie in the boot." On the paranoid gothic, see Eve Kosofsky Sedgwick, *Between Men: English Literature and Male Homosocial Desire* (New York: Columbia University Press, 1985), especially chaps. 5 and 6. For another discussion of the role of sexuality in the film, see Elizabeth Alexander, " 'We're Gonna Deconstruct Your Life!' The Making and

Un-making of the Black Bourgeois Patriarch in *Ricochet*," in *Representing Black Men*, ed. Marcellus Blount and George P. Cunningham (New York: Routledge, 1996), 157–71.

28. John Amos, of course, played the dad on Norman Lear's *Good Times*, a seventies sitcom set in Chicago's Cabrini Green housing project. His presence here efficiently evokes television's ambiguous relation to African American life: *Good Times* was widely hailed, initially, as an unprecedented depiction of working-class blacks, but is now lamented by black cultural critics as a missed opportunity, because it was effectively taken over by Jimmy Walker's coon-like J.J. and evacuated of its critical edge. See the discussion of the series in *Color Adjustment* (videocassette, 1991), produced, written and directed by Marlon T. Riggs, produced by Vivian Kleiman, distributed by California Newsreel.

29. The film neatly collates oppositional spectatorship with paranoia via an unidentified African American guest on a late night talk show. Nick turns on the television just in time to hear him declare, "We believe that Nicholas Styles is the victim of a conspiracy, and we know who they are: this insidious group that tears down any African American politician that dares to defy their power. We're talking of the Rockefellers and their trilateral commission, who, along with the Zionists, have been putting AIDS virus in vending machines all across this nation."

30. Grant Farred, "No Way Out of the Menaced Society," *Camera Obscura* 35 (1995): 7. The fullest account of white Los Angeles' techniques in policing and surveilling the boundaries of its black and Latino neighborhoods is Mike Davis, *City of Quartz: Excavating the Future in Los Angeles* (New York: Vintage, 1992).

31. Paula Massood, "*Menace II Society*," *Cineaste* 20, no. 2 (1993): 44.

32. Chana Kai Lee, *For Freedom's Sake: The Life of Fannie Lou Hamer* (Urbana: University of Illinois Press, 1999), 89; Kay Mills, *This Little Light of Mine: The Life of Fannie Lou Hamer* (New York: Dutton, 1993), 123; and John Lewis with Michael D'Orso, *Walking with the Wind: A Memoir of the Movement* (New York: Simon & Schuster, 1998), 279–80.

Selected Bibliography

Alexander, Elizabeth. *The Venus Hottentot*. Charlottesville and London: University Press of Virginia, 1990.

———. " 'We're Gonna Deconstruct Your Life!' The Making and Un-Making of the Black Bourgeois Patriarch in *Ricochet*." In *Representing Black Men*, edited by Marcellus Blount and George Philbert Cunningham, 157–71. New York: Routledge, 1996.

"American Women: A Century of Change — What's Next?" Washington, D.C.: The Women's Research and Education Institute, 1998.

Anderson, Christopher. *Hollywood TV: The Studio System in the Fifties*. Austin: University of Texas Press, 1994.

Ashmore, Harry S. *Hearts and Minds: The Anatomy of Racism from Roosevelt to Reagan*. New York: McGraw-Hill, 1982.

———. *Civil Rights and Wrongs: A Memoir of Race and Politics, 1944–1994*. New York: Pantheon, 1994.

Bell, Derrick. "Serving Two Masters: Integration Ideals and Client Interests in School Desegregation Legislation." In *Critical Race Theory: The Key Writings That Formed the Movement*, edited by Kimberlé Creshaw, Neil Gotanda, Gary Peller, and Kendall Thomas, 5–19. New York: New Press, 1995.

Berlant, Lauren. "National Brands/National Bodies: *Imitation of Life*." In *The Phantom Public Sphere*, edited by Bruce Robbins, 173–209. Minneapolis: University of Minnesota Press, 1993.

———. *The Queen of America Goes to Washington City: Essays on Sex and Citizenship*. Durham: Duke University Press, 1997.

Boddy, William. *Fifties Television: The Medium and Its Critics*. Urbana and Chicago: University of Illinois Press, 1990.

Bogle, Donald. *Toms, Coons, Mulattoes, Mammies, and Bucks: An Interpretive History of Blacks in American Film*. New rev. ed. New York: Continuum, 1991.

Branch, Taylor. *Parting the Waters: America in the King Years, 1954–1963*. New York: Simon & Schuster, 1988.

———. *Pillar of Fire: American in the King Years, 1963–65*. New York: Simon & Schuster, 1998.

Brinkley, David. *11 Presidents, 4 Wars, 22 Political Conventions, 1 Moon Landing, 3 Assassinations, 2,000 Weeks of News and Other Stuff on Television and 18 Years of Growing up in North Carolina*. New York: Knopf; Distributed by Random House, 1995.

Brunsdon, Charlotte. "Structure of Anxiety: Recent British Television Crime Fiction." *Screen* 39, no. 3 (1998): 223–43.

Burns, Stewart. *Daybreak of Freedom: The Montgomery Bus Boycott*. Chapel Hill: University of North Carolina Press, 1997.

Butler, Judith. "Endangered/Endangering: Schematic Racism and White Paranoia." In *Reading Rodney King/Reading Urban Uprising*, edited by Robert Gooding-Williams, 15–22. New York: Routledge, 1993.

Chestnut, J. L. *Black in Selma: The Uncommon Life of J.L. Chestnut, Jr.* New York: Farrar, Straus and Giroux, 1990.

Classen, Steven. "Broadcast Law and Segregation: A Social History of the WLBT Case." Ph.D. diss., University of Wisconsin, Madison, 1995.

Cone, James H. *Martin & Malcolm & America: A Dream or a Nightmare.* Maryknoll, N.Y.: Orbis, 1991.

Crenshaw, Kimberlé, and Gary Peller. "Reel Time/Real Justice." In *Reading Rodney King/Reading Urban Uprising*, edited by Robert Gooding-Williams, 56–70. New York: Routledge, 1993.

Cripps, Thomas. "*Amos 'n' Andy* and the Debate over American Racial Integration." In *American History/American Television: Interpreting the Video Past*, edited by John E. O'Connor, 33–54. New York: Ungar, 1983.

———. *Making Movies Black: The Hollywood Message Movie from World War II to the Civil Rights Era.* New York: Oxford University Press, 1993.

Crouch, Stanley. *The All-American Skin Game, or, the Decoy of Race: The Long and the Short of It, 1990–1994.* New York: Pantheon, 1995.

Curtin, Michael. *Redeeming the Wasteland: Television Documentary and Cold War Politics.* New Brunswick: Rutgers University Press, 1995.

Dates, Jannette L., and William Barlow, eds. *Split Image: African Americans in the Mass Media.* Washington, D.C.: Howard University Press, 1990.

Dayan, Daniel, and Elihu Katz. *Media Events: The Live Broadcasting of History.* Cambridge: Harvard University Press, 1992.

Delany, Samuel R. *Times Square Red, Times Square Blue.* New York: New York University Press, 1999.

Deming, Robert H. "*Kate and Allie*: 'New Women' and the Audience's Television Archives." In *Private Screenings*, edited by Lynn Spigel and Denise Mann, 203–16. Minneapolis: University of Minnesota Press, 1992.

Dienst, Richard. *Still Life in Real Time: Theory after Television.* Durham: Duke University Press, 1994.

Doane, Mary Ann. "Information, Crisis, Catastrophe." In *Logics of Television*, edited by Patricia Mellencamp, 222–39. Bloomington: Indiana University Press, 1990.

Donovan, Robert J., and Ray Scherer. *Unsilent Revolution: Television News and American Public Life, 1948–1991.* Cambridge: Cambridge University Press, 1992.

Dyer, Richard. *White.* New York: Routledge, 1997.

Dyson, Michael Eric. "Martin and Malcolm." *Transition* 56 (1992): 48–59.

Ely, Melvin Patrick. *The Adventures of Amos 'n' Andy: A Social History of an American Phenomenon.* New York: Free Press, 1991.

Eskew, Glenn T. *But for Birmingham: The Local and National Movements in the Civil Rights Struggle.* Chapel Hill: University of North Carolina Press, 1997.

Fager, Charles E. *Selma, 1965.* New York: Scribner, 1974.

Fairclough, Adam. *To Redeem the Soul of America: The Southern Christian Leadership Conference and Martin Luther King, Jr.* Athens: University of Georgia Press, 1987.

Farber, David. "The Silent Majority and Talk About Revolution." In *The Sixties: From Memory to History*, edited by David Farber, 291–316. Chapel Hill: University of North Carolina Press, 1994.

Farred, Grant. "No Way out of the Menaced Society." *Camera Obscura* 35 (1995): 6–23.

Feuer, Jane. "The Concept of Live Television: Ontology as Ideology." In *Regarding Television—Critical Approaches: An Anthology*, edited by E. Ann Kaplan, 12–22. Frederick, Md.: University Publications of America, 1983.

Frank, Reuven. *Out of Thin Air: The Brief Wonderful Life of Network News.* New York: Simon & Shuster, 1991.

Garrow, David J. *Protest at Selma: Martin Luther King, Jr., and the Voting Rights Act of 1965.* New Haven: Yale University Press, 1978.

———. *Bearing the Cross: Martin Luther King, Jr., and the Southern Christian Leadership Conference.* New York: Vintage, 1988.

———, ed. *The Walking City: The Montgomery Bus Boycott, 1955–1956.* Edited by David J. Garrow. Brooklyn: Carlson, 1989.

Gates, Henry Louis, Jr. "Generation X: A Conversation with Spike Lee and Henry Louis Gates." *Transition* 56 (1992): 176–90.

———. *Colored People: A Memoir.* New York: Knopf, 1994.

George, Lynell. *No Crystal Stair: African-Americans in the City of Angels.* New York: Verso, 1992.

Gitlin, Todd. *The Whole World Is Watching: Mass Media in the Making and Unmaking of the New Left.* Berkeley: University of California Press, 1980.

———. *Inside Prime Time.* Berkeley: University of California Press, 2000.

Goldsby, Jacqueline. "The High and Low Tech of It: The Meaning of Lynching and the Death of Emmett Till." *Yale Journal of Criticism* 9, no. 2 (1996): 245–82.

Good, Paul. *The Trouble I've Seen: White Journalist/Black Movement.* Washington, D.C.: Howard University Press, 1975.

Grant, Judith. "Prime Time Crime: Television Portrayals of Law Enforcement." *Journal of American Culture* 15, no. 1 (1992): 57–68.

Gray, Herman. "Television, Black Americans, and the American Dream." *Critical Studies in Mass Communication* 6 (1989): 376–86.

———. *Watching Race: Television and the Struggle for "Blackness."* Minneapolis: University of Minnesota Press, 1995.

———. "Remembering Civil Rights: Television Memory and the 1960s." In *The Revolution Wasn't Televised: Sixties Television and Social Conflict*, edited by Lynn Spigel and Michael Curtin, 348–58. New York: Routledge, 1997.

Halberstam, David. *The Fifties.* New York: Villard, 1993.

———. *The Children.* New York: Random House, 1998.

Harper, Phillip Brian. "Extra-Special Effects: Televisual Representation and the Claims of the 'Black Experience.'" In *Living Color: Race and Television in the United States*, edited by Sasha Torres, 62–81. Durham: Duke University Press, 1998.

Heath, Stephen. "Representing Television." In *Logics of Television*, edited by Patricia Mellencamp, 267–302. Bloomington: Indiana University Press, 1990.

Heath, Stephen, and Gillian Skirrow. "Television: A World in Action." *Screen* 18, no. 2 (1977): 7–59.

hooks, bell. *Yearning: Race, Gender and Cultural Politics*. Boston: South End, 1990.

———. "Male Heroes and Female Sex Objects: Sexism in Spike Lee's *Malcolm X*." *Cineaste* 19, no. 4 (1993): 13–15.

Hughes Wright, Roberta. *The Birth of the Montgomery Bus Boycott*. Southfield, Mich.: Charro, 1991.

Kellogg, Charles Flint. *NAACP: A History of the National Association for the Advancement of Colored People*. Vol. 1. Baltimore: Johns Hopkins University Press, 1967.

Kelley, Robin D. G. "House Negroes on the Loose: Malcolm X and the Black Bourgeoisie." *Callaloo* 21, no. 2 (1998): 419–35.

King, Mary. *Freedom Song: A Personal Story of the 1960s Civil Rights Movement*. New York: Morrow, 1987.

Lee, Chana Kai. *For Freedom's Sake: The Life of Fannie Lou Hamer*. Urbana: University of Illinois Press, 1999.

Lee, Spike, and Ralph Wiley. *By Any Means Necessary: The Trials and Tribulations of the Making of Malcolm X*. New York: Hyperion, 1992.

Leonard, Thomas C. "Antislavery, Civil Rights, and Incendiary Material." In *Media and Revolution: Comparative Perspectives*, edited by Jeremy D. Popkin, Jr., 115–35. Lexington: University Press of Kentucky, 1995.

Lewis, John, with Michael D'Orso. *Walking with the Wind: A Memoir of the Movement*. New York: Simon & Schuster, 1998.

Lomax, Louis. *When the Word Is Given: A Report on Elijah Muhammad, Malcolm X and the Black Muslim World*. Cleveland and New York: World, 1963.

Longenecker, Stephen L. *Selma's Peacemaker: Ralph Smeltzer and Civil Rights Mediation*. Philadelphia: Temple University Press, 1987.

MacDonald, J. Fred. *Blacks and White TV: African Americans in Television since 1948*. 2nd ed. Chicago: Nelson Hall, 1992.

Manis, Andrew Michael. *A Fire You Can't Put Out: The Civil Rights Life of Birmingham's Reverend Fred Shuttlesworth*. Tuscaloosa: University of Alabama Press, 1999.

Massood, Paula. "*Menace II Society*." *Cineaste* 20, no. 2 (1993): 44–45.

Massood, Paula J. "Mapping the Hood: The Genealogy of City Space in *Boyz N the Hood* and *Menace II Society*." *Cinema Journal* 35, no. 2 (1996): 85–97.

Mauer, Mark, and Tracy Huling. *Young Black Americans and the Criminal Justice System*. Washington, D.C.: The Sentencing Project, 1994.

Mayne, Judith. "*L.A. Law* and Prime-Time Feminism." *Discourse* X, no. 2 (1988): 30–47.

McKelley, James. "Raising Caine in a Down Eden: *Menace II Society* and the Death of Signifyin(G)." *Screen* 39, no. 1 (1998): 36–52.

Mellencamp, Patricia. "TV Time and Catastrophe, or *Beyond the Pleasure Principle* of Television." In *Logics of Television*, edited by Patricia Mellencamp, 240–67. Bloomington: Indiana University Press, 1990.

Mills, Kay. *This Little Light of Mine: The Life of Fannie Lou Hamer*. New York: Dutton, 1993.

Morse, Margaret. "Talk, Talk, Talk: The Space of Discourse in Television News, Sportscasts, Talk Shows and Advertising," *Screen* 26 (1985): 2–15.

Muñoz, José. *Disidentifications: Queers of Color and the Performance of Politics*. Minneapolis: University of Minnesota Press, 1999.

Nunnelley, William A. *Bull Connor*. Tuscaloosa: University of Alabama Press, 1991.

Peller, Gary. "Race-Consciousness." In *Critical Race Theory: The Key Writings That Formed the Movement*, edited by Kimberlé Creshaw, Neil Gotanda, Gary Peller, and Kendall Thomas, 127–58. New York: New Press, 1995.

Raines, Howell. *My Soul Is Rested: Movement Days in the Deep South Remembered*. New York: Penguin, 1983.

Rather, Dan, and Mickey Herskowitz. *The Camera Never Blinks: Adventures of a TV Journalist*. New York: Morrow, 1977.

Reeves, Jimmie L., and Richard Campbell. *Cracked Coverage: Television News, the Anti-Cocaine Crusade, and the Reagan Legacy*. Durham: Duke University Press, 1994.

Robinson, Jo Ann Gibson. *The Montgomery Bus Boycott and the Women Who Started It: The Memoir of Jo Ann Gibson Robinson*. Knoxville: University of Tennessee Press, 1987.

Rooks, Noliwe. "By Any Other Name: *Sweet Justice*, Cicely Tyson, and Contemporary Racial Politics." *Camera Obscura*, no. 36 (1995): 49–66.

Schonfeld, Reese. "The Unsung Heroes of TV News." *Channels* (March–April 1983).

Sedgwick, Eve Kosofsky. *Epistemology of the Closet*. Berkeley: University of California Press, 1990.

Simmons, Ron, and Marlon Riggs. "Sexuality, Television and Death: A Black Gay Dialogue on Malcolm X." In *Malcolm X in Our Own Image*, edited by Joe Wood, 135–54. New York: St. Martin's, 1992.

Smith, Howard K. *Events Leading Up to My Death: The Life of a Twentieth Century Reporter*. New York: St. Martin's, 1996.

Smith, Neil. "Giuliani Time: The Revanchist 1990s." *Social Text* 16, no. 4 (1998): 1–20.

Stanton, Mary. *From Selma to Sorrow: The Life and Death of Viola Liuzzo*. Athens: University of Georgia Press, 1998.

Turim, Maureen. *Flashbacks in Film: Memory & History*. New York: Routledge, 1989.

Turner, Patricia A. *Ceramic Uncles and Celluloid Mammies: Black Images and Their Influences on Culture*. New York: Anchor, 1994.

Warner, Michael. "The Mass Public and the Mass Subject." In *The Phantom Public Sphere*, edited by Bruce Robbins, 234–57. Minneapolis: University of Minnesota Press, 1993.

Watson, Mary Ann. *The Expanding Vista: American Television in the Kennedy Years*. Durham: Duke University Press, 1994.

Webb, Sheyann, Rachel West Nelson, and Frank Sikora. *Selma, Lord, Selma: Girlhood Memories of the Civil-Rights Days*. Tuscaloosa: University of Alabama Press, 1980.

White, Mimi. "Crossing Wavelengths: The Diegetic and Referential Imaginary of American Commercial Television." *Cinema Journal* 25, no. 2 (1986): 51–64.

Whitfield, Stephen J. *A Death in the Delta: The Story of Emmett Till.* Baltimore: Johns Hopkins University Press, 1991.

Williams, Patricia J. "The Rules of the Game." In *Reading Rodney King/Reading Urban Uprising*, edited by Robert Gooding-Williams, 51–55. New York: Routledge, 1993.

Williams, Raymond. *Television: Technology and Cultural Form.* New York: Schocken, 1975.

Williams, Rhonda. "Accumulation as Evisceration: Urban Rebellion and the New Growth Dynamics." In *Reading Rodney King/Reading Urban Uprising*, edited by Robert Gooding-William, 82–97. New York: Routledge, 1993.

Willis, Sharon. *High Contrast: Race and Gender in Contemporary Hollywood Film.* Durham: Duke University Press, 1997.

Wood, Joe. *Malcolm X: In Our Own Image.* New York: St. Martin's, 1992.

X, Malcolm. "Message to the Grass Roots." In *Malcolm X Speaks: Selected Speeches and Statements*, edited by George Breitman, 3–17. New York: Pathfinder, 1993.

Young, Andrew. *A Way Out of No Way: The Spiritual Memoirs of Andrew Young.* Nashville: T. Nelson, 1994.

———. *An Easy Burden: The Civil Rights Movement and the Transformation of America.* New York: HarperCollins, 1996.

Index

Made in the USA
Monee, IL
12 February 2020